W9-AXY-819

WITHDRAWN

Albert Einstein

GIANTS OF SCIENCE

Leonardo da Vinci

Isaac Newton

Sigmund Freud

Marie Curie

Albert Einstein

GIANTS OF SCIENCE

Albert Einstein

By Kathleen Krull

Illustrated by Boris Kulikov

Viking

VIKING

Published by Penguin Group

Penguin Young Readers Group, 345 Hudson Street, New York, New York 10014, U.S.A.

Penguin Group (Canada), 90 Eglinton Avenue East, Suite 700, Toronto, Ontario, Canada M4P 2Y3
(a division of Pearson Penguin Canada Inc.)

Penguin Books Ltd, 80 Strand, London WC2R 0RL, England

Penguin Ireland, 25 St Stephen's Green, Dublin 2, Ireland (a division of Penguin Books Ltd)

Penguin Group (Australia), 250 Camberwell Road, Camberwell, Victoria 3124, Australia
(a division of Pearson Australia Group Pty Ltd)

Penguin Books India Pvt Ltd, 11 Community Centre, Panchsheel Park, New Delhi - 110 017, India

Penguin Group (NZ), Cnr Airborne and Rosedale Roads, Albany, Auckland 1310, New Zealand
(a division of Pearson New Zealand Ltd)

Penguin Books (South Africa) (Pty) Ltd, 24 Sturdee Avenue, Rosebank, Johannesburg 2196, South Africa

Penguin Books Ltd, Registered Offices: 80 Strand, London WC2R 0RL, England

First published in 2009 by Viking, a division of Penguin Young Readers Group

3 5 7 9 10 8 6 4 2

Text copyright © Kathleen Krull, 2009
Illustrations copyright © Boris Kulikov, 2009
All rights reserved

LIBRARY OF CONGRESS CATALOGING-IN-PUBLICATION DATA
Krull, Kathleen.
Albert Einstein / by Kathleen Krull ; illustrated by Boris Kulikov.
p. cm.— (Giants of science)
ISBN 978-0-670-06332-1 (hardcover)
1. Einstein, Albert, 1879–1955—Juvenile literature.
2. Physicists—Biography—Juvenile literature. I. Kulikov, Boris, 1966- ill. II. Title.
QC16.E5K75 2010
530.092—dc22
[B]
2009016037

Printed in U.S.A.   ·   Set in KennerlyH   ·   Book design by Jim Hoover

To Cindy Clevenger and all the Rabbits
—K.K.

ACKNOWLEDGMENTS
Special thanks to David Pascal, Janet Pascal,
Dr. Helen Foster James and Dr. Robert James,
Anatoli Ignatov, Robert Burnham and Patricia
Laughlin, Paul Brewer, Kathryn Hewitt,
and especially Jane O'Connor.

CONTENTS

Albert
Einstein

INTRODUCTION

> "If I have seen further [than other people]
> it is by standing upon the shoulders of giants."
>
> —Isaac Newton, 1675

*A*LBERT EINSTEIN HAD major bedhead. His hair looked as though he'd stuck a finger in an electrical socket. Besides being fashion-challenged, he had problems with school, women, money, memory, and day-to-day life. In the lab, things around him tended to explode. For years no university would have anything to do with him. For years he toiled as a clerk in a government job.

But he had his charms. He became king of the snappy sound bite, always bemused, sort of cuddly, with soulful eyes. And quite rightfully, his name has become a synonym for genius. His work in physics, the science that studies the behavior of objects in motion, was revolutionary. At age twenty-six, in 1905, this man changed the course of the world with his theory of relativity and his famous equation $E = mc^2$. Energy and matter, he said, were basically the same thing, and you could convert one into the other. It is no exaggeration to talk of a pre-Einstein and a post-Einstein world.

Einstein lived in an extraordinary time. The dawn of the twentieth century had a vibe similar to the Renaissance in Italy in the fifteenth century. Civilization seemed to take a giant leap forward. Pablo Picasso reinvented painting with fractured Cubism; Sigmund Freud was charting illnesses not of the body but of the mind; James Joyce wrote novels in a new stream-of-consciousness style; Arnold Schoenberg composed atonal music with no interest in conventional harmony.

Questioning basic concepts in physics? Einstein jumped right in, fueled by his curiosity. "I have no special talents," he once said. "I am only passionately curious."

Science was a solitary pursuit to Einstein. He liked to be alone, free to think for hours on end. In fact, he thought (half-seriously) that scientists should work as lighthouse-keepers, so they would be totally undisturbed. But Einstein was no reclusive, ivory-tower genius. He had lots of help from the very beginning—two supportive parents, one inspirational uncle. Among his best friends were brilliant scientists who loved and nourished him. He even married one of them—Mileva Maric, a fellow physics student.

The Einstein family business was supplying a new technology—electricity—so towns could turn their gas-lights off and glow with electric light. Einstein grew up surrounded by the latest information about using electricity. And he spent seven years working at a patent office in Switzerland, determining whether inventions submitted were truly new or not. He was fortunate that his boss looked the other way when he pulled out his own science theories to work on.

Once, with another scientist, he did invent a type of refrigerator. But newfangled gadgets that made everyday life easier weren't his passion. From his teens, Einstein was obsessed with the big abstract questions—namely, how did the universe work? His whole aim in life, the needle on his compass, was to generalize, to unify, to link together concepts: "It is a glorious feeling to discover the unity of a set of phenomena that seem at first to be completely separate."

His patience was legendary. "The whole of science is nothing more than a refinement of everyday thinking," he said, no matter how long that refinement might take. After spending *ten years* pondering the question of what happens at the speed of light, Einstein found his solutions.

The four papers he published in 1905 revolutionized scientists' understanding of the universe. Space and time no longer meant what people thought they meant; they behaved in ways that didn't seem to agree with common sense. Scientists are *still* working on the implications of all he discovered.

It was a "miracle year" for Einstein, resembling what the great Isaac Newton had experienced in 1666. During that year Newton, a mighty thinker himself, was able to lay down the laws of motion, to understand that the force of gravity that made an apple fall to Earth was the exact same force that pulled the planets around the sun in steady orbits. Newton too saw patterns—but Einstein went much further. It wasn't that Newton was wrong. His way of looking at the world was useful, up to a point. But Einstein was able to pull back a curtain that revealed the limits of Newton's laws.

Like Newton, Einstein seemed to experience

"eureka" moments—"It is a sudden illumination, almost a rapture," he wrote of solving problems. But his discoveries unfurled from long years of thinking and discussing those thoughts with his wife and close friends. As he put it, "Intuition is nothing but the outcome of earlier intellectual experiences." And by "earlier intellectual experiences" he wasn't referring solely to his own.

He stood on the sturdy shoulders of past scientists. Sturdiest of all were Newton's—he provided the foundation of physics with his principles of gravity, mass, motion, and force. As Einstein jokingly described the early history of physics: "In the beginning (if there was such a thing) God created Newton's laws of motion together with the necessary masses and forces." For a couple of centuries, Newton's laws had sufficed nicely to explain everything. But science was expanding way beyond what Newton knew—going to extremes. At these outer limits, things like time seemed to behave illogically. What Einstein discovered cracked apart Newton's dominance.

Like the ancient Greek philosophers, Einstein was more interested in ideas than in testing these ideas through experiments. Marie Curie had spent years in a lab isolating an unknown element—radium. Instead of a lab, Einstein worked inside his head, doing thought experiments, using the deductive method to reach his theories. "The scientist has to worm these general principles out of nature," he stated. As a theoretical physicist, he suggested experiments for others to do to test his theories. His wasn't the usual scientific method, but Einstein wasn't the usual genius.

As for scientists who stand on his shoulders—it is no exaggeration to say that *everyone* sees further because of Einstein's work. As one example, there is a direct line leading from his theory of relativity to the development of the atom bomb, something he passionately wished had never been created. For the most part, his work touches modern life more benignly, from TV and GPS (Global Positioning Systems) to lasers and space travel . . . and that electric eye that opens the supermarket door when you approach. Thank Einstein for that.

Physics is hard stuff, all about forces such as gravity and magnetism that you can't see. You can go through everyday life without paying attention to physics, and yet it governs the universe, including every move you make—fascinating. And just about all of it is explained by Einstein's equations—from the smallest event (tiny particles in motion) to the largest (the expanding universe). His ideas make your head spin, in a down-the-rabbit-hole, *Alice in Wonderland* sort of way.

But Einstein did us a favor by thinking in pictures. And through his imagery—falling elevators, speeding trains, moving clocks, riding a beam of light, falling backward out of a chair, beetles crawling over a branch—it becomes easier for us less-than-geniuses to understand what he's explaining. His ability to make visual analogies was one of his greatest strengths.

As for other strengths, he had many. Like Newton, he always kept the curiosity of a child; while at work he thought of himself as a boy happily playing. He was never afraid to try a new approach. "Imagination is more important than knowledge," he insisted.

He wasn't afraid to fail, and he was vigilant about finding and fixing his mistakes. (He did make them.) Long after he'd become an icon, a celebrity genius, he ruefully confessed, "I am no Einstein."

CHAPTER ONE

That Boy in the Back of the Classroom

*L*ITTLE ALBERT EINSTEIN was no model child. For starters, there was his temper. At age five he threw a chair at a tutor, who quit on the spot. He also threw things at Maja, his little sister. "It takes a sound skull to be the sister of an intellectual," Maja later said diplomatically. (They became close as grown-ups.)

He wasn't chatty or sociable. He liked to go his own way. Expressing things in words didn't come naturally to him. Instead, his head was full of pictures. He started talking much later than most children. Even then he spoke in a quirky fashion, whispering something to himself, sometimes several times, before saying it out loud. Behind his back, the family maid referred to him as "the dopey one."

He was born on March 14, 1879, in the southwestern corner of Germany known as Swabia. The small town of Ulm prospered, set amid gently rolling hills and long stretches of river where men caught fish on the beautiful blue waters of the Danube. Einstein's parents were not fishermen but merchants—ambitious people who valued education and accomplishment. Their son's late development so worried them that they started taking him to doctors to see what was wrong.

Einstein's father, Hermann, was good at math and had been to high school, though his family couldn't afford to send him to college. He became a salesman—not a particularly good one—who sold featherbeds. Then he moved his family to Munich and went into business with his brother Jakob, an engineer and successful inventor. Together they started up a gas and electrical supply company. They could see that electricity was clearly the future.

Three years later came electric lighting—first displayed by New Jersey's Thomas Edison in the very year of Einstein's birth. The first city in Germany to see streetlamps light up electrically was Munich, where the Einstein family was now living.

Hermann Einstein's job was to win contracts to provide other German towns with lighting. The Einstein brothers faced serious competition, however, and mild, good-natured Hermann was still no crack salesman.

Albert's mother, Pauline, came from a wealthy family that kept the Einsteins respectable even when times were tough. She ran the household. "Keeping busy brings blessings" was a proverb that she embroidered on the family tablecloth—and busy she was. She encouraged Albert to be independent and self-sufficient. Even when he was very young, she would drop him off on a busy Munich street and let him find his own way home (secretly shadowing him all the while).

The doctors who examined young Albert couldn't find anything wrong. Some modern doctors have suggested labels of Asperger's syndrome or another disorder on the autism spectrum, though the evidence to support this diagnosis is slim. Still, even as an adult he tended to repeat things, especially if they were funny. Today he might be diagnosed with a mild form of a verbal disorder called echolalia.

"I developed so slowly," he said later, by which time

he had decided that this was a plus, not a minus. He believed it gave him more time than the average child had to observe the world, so that even as an adult he was able to look freshly at basic things, such as space and time. And always pictures, not words, continued to fill his head. "I very rarely think in words at all," he once remarked. "A thought comes, and I may try to express it in words afterwards."

Some of Einstein's first words were "Yes, but where are the wheels?"—spoken when he was three. He was greeting his newborn sister, Maja, who he'd been told was a new toy.

He loved his toys, especially a marvelous small steam-driven engine given to him by a generous uncle. He spent all of his playtime alone with toys, daydreaming. (A governess called him "Father Bore.") Instead of doing things with other children, he preferred playing with his puzzles, a complicated set of stone building blocks, and decks of cards. Maja bragged that he was able to make card structures fourteen stories high— evidence of a boy with unusual patience.

A good pianist, Einstein's mother, Pauline, made her son take violin lessons. He was soon playing classical duets with her. He never cared for Beethoven (too emotional), but he adored Bach, Schubert, and most of all, the elegant structures of Mozart's music, "so pure it seems to have been ever-present in the universe." Reports vary about the quality of Einstein's playing, but throughout his life music helped him think. When a problem was stumping him, even in the middle of the night, he would take up his violin and soar to a solution.

His interest in science was first kindled at age four or five. He was sick in bed and his father brought him a compass to play with. Einstein couldn't stop turning it around: Why did its magnetized needle always point north, no matter how he tilted it? His dad could provide no satisfactory explanation. Compasses had been around for at least a thousand years, first invented by Chinese scholars. But Einstein wanted to know *how* the magnetism crossed space into his own home, and that his father couldn't say.

Holding the compass, Einstein got so excited that he was literally shaking.

That compass, he said later, was the source of his lifelong sense of wonder about invisible forces at work in the universe: "This experience made a deep and lasting impression on me—something deeply hidden had to be behind things." In later life it led to his obsession

with what that *one* "something" was. He searched to find a unified theory, a mathematical way to explain *everything* in the universe. One thing is for certain—Einstein never thought small.

His uncle Jakob was a scientific thinker too, although someone more interested in the practical applications of electricity. Over the years, Jakob obtained patents (official papers that grant someone the sole right to sell or make an invention) for electric meters, circuit breakers, new types of lamps, new ways to spin wire coils, and new ways of moving magnets to build electric generators.

In Munich every fall, there is a gigantic citywide folk festival called Oktoberfest. When Albert was six, the Oktoberfest party was lit up for the first time with electric lights, thanks to the Einstein brothers' company. At one point the company, with two hundred employees, rivaled the other major power companies, including the mighty Siemens Company.

Einstein started school the same year as that memorable Oktoberfest. His parents, though Jewish, preferred the local Catholic school for Albert because it was close to home and he could walk there. To him, the school seemed designed to instill fear, with students getting smacked on the hand with a ruler for every wrong answer. As the only Jewish student, Einstein was sometimes bullied. Jews had been granted citizenship in almost all of Germany by 1867, but the word "anti-Semitism" first appeared in print in German in 1879, the same year Einstein was born—and prejudice against Jews was on the rise. Despite all the frustrations, he was always at the top of his class.

At nine, he went on to the Luitpold Gymnasium, considered a modern German school with an up-to-date lab. It was known for math and science, Latin and Greek, and strict teachers.

Einstein hated it. He hated rote learning, being force-fed facts; he hated the way teachers actively discouraged questions, he hated the military discipline. The teachers were like drill sergeants, the atmosphere too much like the army. (The army was looming soon enough. Like every boy in Germany, Einstein faced compulsory service at age seventeen, and he for one was dreading it.) Einstein never played sports with the other boys, yet he was able to explain weird things to them, such as the way a telephone worked. (He was five when his family got their first phone, and it was like another amazing toy to him.) His fellow students' nicknames for him were variations on "nerd"—"big bore" and "straight arrow."

All his life Einstein remained a harsh critic of the rigid German educational system, which he felt brainwashed students: "When a person can take pleasure in marching in step to a piece of music, it is enough to make me despise him. He has been given his big brain only by mistake."

At home Albert was free to pursue his own education. Cocooning himself within the Einsteins' comfortable, if noisy, house, he forged on, encouraged by his family. His parents bought his school textbooks early, so he could get ahead in math during summer vacations. Uncle Jakob would set up complicated algebra problems, and Albert would sit by himself for days, not going out to play, until he'd finally discover the solutions and experience a genuine thrill.

Besides Uncle Jakob, Einstein had another mentor. Instead of following the traditional Jewish custom of hosting a poor religious student on the Sabbath, the Einsteins hosted a young medical student named Max Talmud on Thursdays. Starting when Einstein was ten, Max became an informal tutor, ever widening the boy's horizons.

Max brought over books that included a popular series called *People's Books on Natural Science*. The author, Aaron Bernstein, related with exhilaration the latest in experiments, emphasizing the unity in science. Repeatedly he wrote about the speed of light, imagining creative trips such as being on a speeding train when a bullet comes through the window, or riding through a telegraph line with an electric signal. Einstein read the series—all twenty-one volumes—with "breathless attention," and he later credited it with shaping his approach as a scientist.

When Albert was twelve, Max gave him a book

of geometry, which he devoured, calling it his "sacred little geometry book." Shapes, angles, lines—what fun.

From math Max moved on to philosophy. He introduced Einstein to Immanuel Kant, the influential German whose *Critique of Pure Reason* was fashionable among intellectuals of the day. In writing about the relationship between reality and the human mind, Kant proposed that reality exists, but only the mind can give it form within the context of space and time. Mathematical principles are one way of providing that context and defining reality. At thirteen, Einstein picked Kant as his favorite philosopher.

A persistent, popular myth has it that Einstein did poorly in school and even failed math. But published copies of his report cards show that he got good grades in everything, including math.

Unfortunately, he was not cool about concealing his impatience with teachers. He had no tolerance for fools, whether they were in positions of authority or not. "Blind respect for authority is the greatest enemy of truth," he said later, and it was impossible for him to fake that respect.

His attitude naturally infuriated and provoked teachers. One even told him that he would never amount to anything. Another "uninvited" Einstein to class. When Einstein protested that he hadn't done anything to deserve the ban, the teacher accused him of always sitting in the back row, smirking. He set a terrible example for the other boys.

His experience at Luitpold Gymnasium reinforced his determination to go it alone, to remove himself from authority. It was a trait that dominated his life and played a part in his discoveries. It could be argued, in fact, that attending rigid German schools honed and perfected Einstein's natural instinct to become a rebellious, independent thinker.

By the time he was fifteen, working on his own, he was focused on science, especially physics, with its absorbing new ideas about magnetism and electricity and light. Later he said that this was the year he became "convinced that nature could be understood as a relatively simple mathematical structure." Not that he had a clue right then what that structure was.

Also when he was fifteen, he quit Luitpold—even though he had three years left before graduation.

CHAPTER TWO

The Dropout

*I*T'S ALWAYS BEEN hazy whether Einstein left high school by choice or was asked to leave. During Christmas break, he prevailed upon his family doctor to write a note saying that he was suffering from nervous exhaustion. Einstein gave it to the school and simply didn't go back after Christmas vacation. There is no record of any teacher begging him to reconsider.

Besides hating the school, he had another motive to drop out. The family's fortunes had turned sour. Three years earlier, in 1891, eight of Uncle Jakob's dynamos had gone on display at the International Electrical Exhibition in Frankfurt. They were seen by more than a

million people, excited at the sneak preview of the won-
ders electricity would bring to daily life. But since then
the Einstein family business had been losing important
contracts. By 1894, the business was failing.

The Einstein brothers decided to head for Milan,
Italy, for what they hoped were better job opportuni-
ties. Hermann sold the lovely family house, and everyone except Albert packed up and moved to Italy. He
was left behind with relatives in order to finish his
education.

He felt abandoned, and was also alarmed by the
prospect of military duty. So he escaped. With no particular symptoms of nervous exhaustion, he hopped on
a train to Italy, crossed the Alps, and surprised his
parents.

They were surprised all right—and distressed,
foreseeing as he didn't the problems facing a high-school
dropout with no job skills. Since he hadn't finished the
Luitpold, there was no chance of Albert attending any
of the prestigious European universities nearby. His
prospects couldn't have looked less promising.

But he started helping out with the Einstein family business. Everyone noticed how much Albert knew
about electricity and magnets. Albert's father tried to
talk him into studying to become an engineer like his

uncle Jakob, but that choice didn't set off any sparks. He did love Italy and spent days alone hiking in the Alps doing what came most easily to him: thinking, thinking, and more thinking.

He kept his nervous parents appeased by promising to study on his own and apply to a technical college. He bought three volumes of an advanced physics textbook and plowed through them, making many notes in the margins. Even in the midst of a boisterous family gathering, he would put in productive study time on the couch.

At sixteen, on his own, he wrote his first theoretical physics essay, about magnetic fields, which he proudly mailed off to an uncle on his mother's side. And even though he was two years shy of the required age, Einstein pounced on the chance to apply directly to the Zürich Polytechnic School in Switzerland. If he could pass its stiff entrance examinations, this technical and teachers college would admit him even without a high school diploma. He aced mathematics and physics, but he failed at French, literature, zoology, and botany. Zürich Polytechnic would accept him only on the condition that he first finish his formal schooling.

Fortunately, Albert found a special Swiss school,

a progressive, freethinking school. By himself, Albert moved to Aarau, Switzerland, thirty miles outside of Zürich. He boarded with the family of Jost Winteler, a professor of history and Greek at the school.

The Winteler family and Einstein became close friends. He grew more sociable and sometimes joined their dinners instead of studying alone. Jost and his wife were like second parents, forever supportive. Of their seven children, the youngest daughter, Marie, was Einstein's first girlfriend. Nowhere near his equal intellectually, she was studying to become a teacher. Marie's brother Paul eventually married Einstein's sister, Maja. The eldest Winteler daughter, Anna, would later marry Einstein's best friend, Michele Besso.

The progressive approach to education was just the opposite of Einstein's old school's—encouraging individuality, thinking visually, using observation to reach conclusions, promoting independent thought. The school had a new physics lab, but Einstein's inclination was still toward thinking in pictures, something he didn't need a lab for.

At sixteen he started thinking about one picture in particular: What would it be like to ride a beam of light? What would the beam look like if you could run alongside it? If you ran as fast as the light, what would happen? These questions were to occupy his mind for the next ten years. It was his first thought experiment—created not in a lab, but inside his own head.

Einstein flourished under the care of the Winteler family, and in 1896 he reapplied to Polytechnic. This time, during the entrance exam, he completed the two-hour physics test with forty-five minutes to spare, earning a higher grade than anyone else. In the other subjects, he did well enough for admission.

It was a thrilling time to be considering a career in science. Electrons, radioactivity, X-rays—these were all spanking-new discoveries. Theoretical physics was the hot field—trying to figure out how the whole universe worked and reduce it to mathematical equations.

By this time, Einstein had renounced his German citizenship. One thing he knew for sure—he disliked all things German, and he wasn't going back. He was thinking vaguely of training at Polytechnic to become a teacher.

He wanted to keep soaring with his thoughts: "Thinking for its own sake [is] like music!"

CHAPTER THREE

Explosions in the Lab

$\mathcal{E}$INSTEIN'S REBEL WAYS persisted at Polytechnic.

He absolutely hated exams because "one had to cram all this stuff into one's mind . . . whether one liked it or not."

And he still bugged his teachers with his condescending attitude. "You'll never let yourself be told anything," the exasperated head of the physics department said to him, predicting that the trait would hinder him despite his obvious intelligence.

That professor, Heinrich Weber, was someone Einstein admired—at least at first. In two years, he took fifteen courses from Weber. But ultimately he grew disenchanted. Weber wasn't progressive and was focused too much on the past. To Einstein's dismay, Weber taught nothing on the important new discoveries in physics of the past forty years.

For Einstein, the crucial thing about physics was solving current puzzles about the universe. In Weber's classes, he was going nowhere with his quest to ride the light beam.

As for the other professor in the physics department, Einstein didn't think enough of him to attend his classes at all. This professor suggested Einstein change majors and flunked him, along with giving him an official reprimand for "lack of diligence."

Surprisingly, Einstein did manage to pass most courses. But in the math department, one professor called him "a lazy dog" because he avoided the challenging classes. And theoretical physics did require lots of advanced math. In later life, Einstein would regret not paying more attention to it.

Polytechnic had just opened an up-to-the-minute lab. When a teacher gave the class a list of instructions for carrying out an experiment, Einstein made a rude show of tossing the list in the trash and starting off in his own way.

Attempting another experiment, he accidentally set off an explosion, nearly blowing himself up. He injured his right hand badly enough to require stitches, preventing him from using a pen or playing his violin for weeks. It was one more experience that led him to prefer thought experiments to real ones.

But even while he was cutting classes, he was studying "with a holy zeal" on his own. In his cheap boardinghouse rooms, he tackled more current physics. He found inspiration in the work of Henri Poincaré, the French mathematician who'd been Marie Curie's old math teacher. Poincaré went so far as to question Newton's beliefs in absolute time and absolute space—a dismissal that Einstein found breathtaking in its boldness.

Concentrating on his own reading kept depression at bay. Often he fretted over his father's continued financial failures and his own inability to help. In one letter he confided to Maja, "I am nothing but a burden to my family. . . . It would be better off if I were not alive at all."

Music remained a source of solace. One story has him entering a total stranger's house when he heard her playing Mozart on the piano—bringing his violin so he could accompany her.

New friends brightened his life. He began hanging out at coffeehouses such as Café Metropole on the banks of the Limmat River. Not a drinker (he dismissed beer as a recipe for stupidity), he sipped iced coffee, ate cheap bratwurst, smoked a pipe (watching the smoke and envisioning it as atoms in action). Sometimes he and his new pals went to musical events. He learned how to sail in the Alpine lakes, scribbling in his notebooks whenever the wind died down. But mostly Albert and his circle of friends talked.

Something about Zürich stimulated talking. A beautiful city nestled among tall green mountains, with plenty of fresh air, a bustling center of commerce. Café life thrived, connecting various movers and shakers from many fields. The city was advanced technologically, fully lit with electricity, with phones installed since 1880, and horse-drawn carriages replaced by electric trams in 1894.

Ultimately Einstein's years in Zürich proved to be happy ones. Some of his new acquaintances became friends for life. Marcel Grossmann, for example—a brilliant mathematician who always believed in Einstein's greatness. As for how Einstein managed to pass courses whose classes he had skipped, he gave credit to the incredibly generous Grossmann, who, before exams, shared his excellent class notes with Einstein.

With another friend, Michele Besso, he enjoyed endless conversations about space and time. Not as focused or ambitious as Einstein, and kind of a bum-bler, Besso was the one who introduced Einstein to the work of Austrian physicist Ernst Mach. Mach, like Poincaré, was questioning the way Newton saw time and space. This fanned the fire of Einstein's own skepticism.

What about romance? His long-distance relation-ship with Marie Winteler was fading. He'd been mail-ing her unromantic baskets of dirty clothes for her to wash and had even stopped including a letter with the laundry.

Polytechnic, however, was one of the few Euro-pean universities open to women. This was where Ein-stein fell head-over-heels in love with a fellow physics student, Mileva Maric. From Novi Sad, a Serbian city then part of Hungary, Mileva had been a child prodigy in math and was a highly unusual woman for her time. With ambitions encouraged by her supportive father, she started as a medical student, then switched to phys-ics in 1896 and enrolled at Polytechnic.

She and Einstein started off with study-dates and later hiked the Alps together.

Their "love letters" were very unconventional. Her first letter to him was all about her excitement at the latest kinetic theory. His letter back to her waxed eloquent about "the electrodynamics of moving bodies." They were clearly on the same page intellectually. Within several months, they were an item.

Her friends had their doubts about sloppy, absent-minded Einstein. What could Mileva see in a man who couldn't care less about clothes or grooming? Didn't it irritate her that he was always losing his keys . . . leaving clothes behind while traveling . . . even forgetting his whole suitcase?

His friends had even stronger reservations about her. The only woman in the physics department, she was still not an obvious choice for a girlfriend. More than three years older than Einstein, she suffered from bouts of tuberculosis, depression, and a limp due to a hip dislocated at birth. She was not considered attractive (some deemed her downright plain), too intense and serious, moody, possessive, prone to jealousy.

But Mileva was very, very smart, and just as passionate about math and science as he was. Here was a peer, someone he could talk to.

They reveled in being bohemians together. He called her Dollie, "my street urchin," and "you little witch." She called him Johnnie and "my wicked little sweetheart." He wrote that "we understand each other's dark souls so well, and also drinking coffee and eating sausages, etcetera." He even made up poems: "Oh my! That Johnnie boy! / So crazy with desire / While thinking of his Dollie / His pillow catches fire." (Writing light verse was something he did—badly—all his life.)

Unlike most men of the time, he was supportive of her studies: "How proud I will be to have a little PhD for a sweetheart," he wrote. In fact, being able to work together made studying "soothing and also less boring." In another letter he wrote that he couldn't wait for the fun they would have on their next hike—"And then we'll start in on Helmholtz's electromagnetic theory of light. . . ."

By 1900, Einstein was set to graduate from Polytechnic. All he owed was a senior thesis to his now-enemy Weber. He wanted to write about the earth's speed as it moved. Unfortunately, Weber rejected his proposal, then his second proposal. Einstein was forced to pick something to Weber's liking, a study of heat conduction, a topic he said later was of "no interest to me."

In his graduating class of five, he ranked fourth.·
Mileva, alas, failed. Einstein jaunted off to the Swiss
Alps without her, to vacation with his family.

Along with him he lugged science tomes, determined
to continue his aggressive program of self-education.
For what he wanted to know, he was clearly going to
have to struggle on alone.

CHAPTER FOUR

An Office Clerk?

ITH HIS USUAL bravado, Einstein assumed that the first item on his postgraduate agenda would be to land an assistant's job at Polytechnic. This would provide money while he continued his independent study. He was anxious to settle down with Mileva and work together with her. But he couldn't marry and support a family without a job.

For someone so smart, he was clueless that alienating his teachers might eventually work against him. The two physics professors at Polytechnic were not exactly his fans. And his math teachers were not swayed by his letter lamely claiming that his reason for cutting so many classes was "lack of time."

So he had to apply to other schools. Months passed while he tried to land an academic job elsewhere. But surprise—none of his professors would write a letter of recommendation, and Weber in particular seemed to be badmouthing him behind his back. Months passed. Einstein later wrote, "I could have found a job long ago had it not been for Weber's underhandedness."

He attempted to pay attention to the Einstein family business, touring new power plants, readying himself to take "Papa's place in an emergency." But his heart wasn't in it. Also, his parents kept badgering him to break up with Mileva. They vehemently opposed the relationship—she was too independent, not respectable enough, and they had concerns about her poor health and their age difference. They doubted she would attend to her "wifely" duties—surely marrying her would ruin his future.

Rebel that he was, Einstein defied his parents.

While Mileva studied, he hung out at her apartment, job-hunting ever more frantically, living on small sums from relatives. He saved his pennies for bikes so they could take bike trips every few weeks and also set aside money to pay the fee for Swiss citizenship. This was important to him—Einstein found Switzerland very "humane" for "its gentle respect for individuals and their privacy." In 1901 he became a citizen. He even dutifully showed up for the required army service but was rejected (for flat, sweaty feet and varicose veins).

That same year, his first published paper came out in the prestigious German journal *Annals of Physics*. The topic was hardly groundbreaking—it was on the capillary effect (the force that makes liquid climb up a drinking straw) and how this related to Newton's laws of gravity. But the paper was noteworthy for taking as fact that molecules and atoms existed, something still not universally accepted. The paper was totally ignored. In any case, it turned out its basic assumption was wrong—yes, even Einstein made mistakes. But at least he could use the paper to beef up the applications he was sending to professors all over Europe.

They were underwhelmed and usually didn't even respond.

Months turned into years. Einstein was turned down for every academic position he applied for. Partly because he was really bad at job applications—tactless, obnoxious, often his own worst enemy. He spent time writing letters to other scientists, pointing out their mistakes—even scientists he hoped to work for. As Mileva admitted, "You know my sweetheart has a sharp tongue." Plus they both suspected that anti-Semitism, on the rise, was a factor in the hiring practices at many universities.

"I leave no stone unturned and do not give up my sense of humor," he said bravely. From his meager funds he took to enclosing a postage-paid postcard with his applications to make it as easy as possible to answer. Later these would become collectible, but at the time they failed to do the trick. Once his father even wrote a desperate plea to a professor behind Einstein's back, trying to help—still with no success.

Einstein kept up with his independent study, always questioning and disputing the work of others. He also wrote long letters to Michele Besso, now an engineer and still his closest friend. Their exchanges on current topics in physics were inspiring him more than anything else.

On his own, he wrote a doctoral dissertation and sent it to Alfred Kleiner, the conservative professor of Experimental Physics at the University of Zürich. This professor liked him personally, and Einstein was minimally complimentary in return. ("He's not quite as stupid as I'd thought," he said.) Kleiner, however, flat-out rejected the dissertation for its attack on established ideas.

Then the family's business finally went bankrupt, and Einstein sank to perhaps the lowest point in his life. He looked for jobs tutoring children. "Trial lessons free of charge," he advertised pathetically, but he was fired from even these jobs. Then Mileva became preg-nant, throwing the couple into a crisis.

Einstein professed to be thrilled, but he never seemed to be around during the pregnancy. While he was vacationing in the Alps, Mileva again failed the exam required to graduate from Polytechnic.

His letters to her express a naïve vision of the three of them—mama, papa, baby—living together "complete-ly undisturbed, and with no one around to tell us what to do!" Then he'd write on and on about cathode rays and electrons. He was not present when the baby girl, Lieserl, was born in January 1902 at her grandparents' home in Novi Sad, Serbia. The plan was for the baby to remain there for the time being.

Six months later, his friend Marcel Grossmann saved him yet again. A job! Grossmann's father recommended Einstein for a government job in Berne, the capital of Switzerland. Quite a respectable job, in fact— an inspection clerk in the Swiss Patent Office. Grossmann actually got the job description rewritten with Einstein in mind. He was to evaluate applications for patents, the papers that grant the right of ownership to an invention. He was no longer aiming to be a professor but was going to work six days a week, eight hours a day, as Technical Expert Class 3 of the Federal Office for Intellectual Property.

The job wasn't the drudgery it may sound like. It entailed scrutinizing patent descriptions for flaws—did the inventions actually work, were they in fact new, did everything make sense? His boss instructed, "When you pick up an application, think that everything the inventor says is wrong." This was a delicious task for a rebel who questioned everything. Plus, the process was familiar to him from his own family: Uncle Jakob had applied for and won many patents.

Part of Einstein's job was to rewrite confusing descriptions, which sharpened his own writing skills. He learned how complex designs could be explained by starting from a few clear principles.

"I enjoy my work at the office very much, because

it is uncommonly diversified," he insisted. (According to myth, he approved the patent for the design of the famous Toblerone chocolate bar.) Many applications had to do with things that genuinely interested him—time, energy, light, and speed—and their applications.

The seven years spent in his office job weren't a complete detour from his scientific work. He could finish up his tasks in two or three hours, then spend time on his own scientific exploration, carrying on his thought experiments. His boss was supportive, although Einstein was careful: "Whenever anybody would come by, I would cram my notes into my desk drawer and pretend to work on my office work."

Einstein's job turned out to be a blessing in disguise. It gave him security and more freedom than he would have had at a university, where he would have been forced to play it safe and publish papers he didn't care about. He called his office "that worldly cloister where I hatched my most beautiful ideas."

Every day he walked to his office, often with his best friend, Besso, who eventually came to work at the patent office too. So twice a day Einstein passed by the symbol of Berne, its medieval clock tower. Bears brandished musical instruments, a rooster flapped its wings, a jester rang bells, an astronomical device tracked the motions of planets, and old Father Time himself appeared, bearing an hourglass. All with cogs, wheels, levers, and chains, the famous clock put on an amazing show of technology every hour.

A nearby train station used this clock to set all the clocks on the platforms. So did the trains arriving from other countries. Countries in Europe were in the process of introducing electrical signals to get clocks in different time zones in sync. Synchronicity was a craze in Switzerland, where clock-making was an art. For Einstein, the bigger, more interesting question was: What did it mean to say things happen at the same time? Many of his later thought experiments were to involve moving trains and clocks.

For further intellectual stimulation, he started a sort of book club with two other scholars. The trio called themselves the Olympia Academy; they went hiking, played tricks on one another, but most of all they read—classics by Sophocles and Cervantes, and some of Einstein's old favorites such as Poincaré and Kant. They would yak for hours sometimes, with Einstein finishing off the evening with a violin solo.

Mileva sometimes appeared at the Academy

meetings, not contributing anything except tea, sausages, cheese, and fruit. But with a steady if small income for the first time in his life, Einstein finally felt confident enough to marry her. Einstein's father became seriously ill and, just before he died, gave his blessing for the marriage. His father's death shocked and depressed Einstein, and for years, he was overcome by regret that his father had died believing him a failure.

The only witnesses to the 1903 wedding were the two other members of the Olympia Academy, who accompanied the bride and groom to a restaurant afterward. (Later when the newlyweds arrived home, Einstein realized that, quite typically, he had forgotten his keys, and had to go wake the landlady.)

What about their daughter, baby Lieserl? She never joined her parents. Having an illegitimate child wasn't all that unusual, but it still wasn't considered respectable, especially for someone with a government job. Most scholars believe that Lieserl was given up for adoption in Serbia and died of scarlet fever in 1903. Einstein never saw his first child. Nor did he ever tell anyone about her. (Not until 1986, when his papers were made public, did scholars learn of her existence.)

As for marriage, Einstein claimed to be dead-set

against having a traditional, boring one. He told Mileva, "You must always be my witch and street urchin. Everyone but you seems foreign to me, as if they were separated from me by an invisible wall." He assumed that he and Mileva would continue to pursue science together. But after failing her second exam and giving up her child, Mileva was losing sight of her goal of being a scholar. She continued to check Einstein's math, help him talk through ideas, serve as his biggest cheerleader, and keep him fed.

Only weeks into the marriage, her role had shrunk to the point where she was mostly keeping him fed. He wrote that "she takes excellent care of everything, cooks well, and is always cheerful." Actually she was growing moodier and more jealous, but he didn't pick up on it. Not yet.

Previously, he may have been supportive of her as a scientist, but now he didn't want her to contribute to his work. "Where you females are concerned, your production center is not situated in the brain," he once told a colleague's wife. For all his talk of equal partners, his attitude toward women in general and toward Mileva in particular was quite typical of a man of his day.

When their son, Hans Albert, was born in 1904,

Einstein was attentive at first. He constructed toys, using strings and matchboxes to make little cars; played
lullabies on his violin; told stories. Yet, as Hans said later, "Even the loudest baby-crying didn't seem to disturb
Father." He'd simply bounce the baby on his knee and
write with the other hand, his thought pictures always
occupying his mind.

That same year, Marie Curie (the role model for
Mileva and every woman scientist in Europe) won the
Nobel Prize with her husband, Pierre. The Curies were
a remarkable husband-and-wife team, one that must have
underscored for Mileva that she was now relegated to
housewife, strapped with childcare and keeping house.

The apartment was full of the odor of diapers boil-
ing and smoke leaking from the stove, a place that was
too cold in winter, hot and extra-smelly in summer. Einstein escaped for long walks, and in his absentminded
fashion, would wander into the countryside by mistake.

CHAPTER FIVE

Finally, Miracles

I N 1905 ALBERT Einstein, at age twenty-six, published four papers in the most important of the science journals, *Annals of Physics*. It is no exaggeration to say that each of them would alter the course of modern physics.

In full creative flower, as revolutionary as anyone, he was still able to be self-mocking. "Some inconsequential babble" was how he described his work in a letter to one of his Olympia Academy buddies, whom he addressed jokingly as "You frozen whale."

The first paper focused on the photoelectric effect, a phenomenon first identified back in 1887. Scientists had observed that when light was aimed at certain metals, the surfaces would emit a stream of particles. They realized that energy from the light was knocking the particles out of the metal. Several things about these particles, however, were puzzling. It was generally accepted that light was a wave. Yet the behavior of these particles didn't fit the theory of how light waves were supposed to work.

Waves of light are described by their intensity and frequency. Intensity refers to the height of the wave and affects how bright a light is. Frequency refers to the length of the wave and affects the color of the light— red light has the lowest frequency of light we can see. So a very bright red light has a high intensity but only a low frequency.

In experiments, scientists found that the number of particles that a metal emitted depended upon only the intensity of the light beam, not the frequency—the more intense the light, the more particles emitted. But below a certain frequency, no matter how intense the light was, no particles were released from the metal. That seemed odd.

On the other hand, how fast the particles moved depended *solely* on the frequency of the light. The higher the frequency, the more energetic the particles were.

This didn't seem to make any sense to Einstein. If light was a wave, then the greater the intensity of the wave, the greater the amount of energy directed at the piece of metal. So as the intensity of the light increased, both the number of the particles knocked out of the metal *and* their speed should increase. Also, an intense light, even at low frequency, should still have enough energy to knock *some* particles out of the metal. But that wasn't happening.

Genius that he was, Einstein explained what seemed illogical by drawing on the work of another great theoretical physicist, Max Planck. Planck had been studying the way objects radiate heat. Heat energy wasn't continuous, he said. It existed in separate little packets (called quanta) in very specific sizes—like a T-shirt that comes in small, medium, and large, with no sizes in between. You could have a packet with a certain amount of energy or a packet with twice that amount, or three times that amount, but nothing in between.

Einstein took Planck's idea about packets of energy and applied it to the beams of light shining on the metals. What if the beam of light was made up of packets of light? High-intensity light would have more packets in it than lower-intensity light. And a higher frequency would increase the amount of energy in each packet. With these assumptions, the results made perfect sense. A certain amount of energy would be needed to knock a particle out of the metal. Each packet would have to have at least that much energy. So until each individual packet was strong enough (that is, the frequency was high enough), it wouldn't matter how many packets you had (that is, how intense the light was)—none of them would be strong enough to knock out a particle. Once the packets were big enough, the more of them you had, the greater the number of particles you would knock out. But since each packet of energy was the same size, each particle would still fly out with the same speed. In order to make the particles fly out faster, you would have to make each packet of energy bigger—increase the frequency—so that the particles got knocked out more energetically.

Between them, Planck and Einstein had begun the branch of modern physics that would come to be called quantum theory. Einstein had also established one confusing feature of physics that is still hard to make sense of today: By looking at light as little quantum packets, he was in effect saying that light was not a wave—it was a stream of particles. But very often, it was necessary to think of light as a wave. In fact, Einstein himself would treat light as a wave later that year in order to come up with the theory of special relativity. So which is it? Scientists now say that light is actually both a wave and particles at the same time—they call it a "wavicle."

In his first paper of 1905, Einstein came up with a good theory explaining the photoelectric effect, the reason why it works as it does. Practical applications of his discovery include TV and many other inventions. And the paper gave a tremendous boost to Planck's quantum theory, which was to dominate physics for the next century.

As was his custom, Einstein presented his theory and left it to others to test with experiments. More than ten years would pass before American Robert Millikan proved Einstein correct in his law of the photoelectric effect; Millikan later won the 1923 Nobel Prize for his work.

At the same time he crafted this famous paper, Einstein was struggling to boost his credibility by earning his doctorate degree. After his first dissertation had been rejected by Alfred Kleiner at the University of Zürich, Einstein tried again. He searched for a "safe" topic, nothing too controversial. He chose to analyze the size of molecules, using those in liquids (instead of gases, as other researchers had done). Perhaps exaggerating, Einstein would later joke that Kleiner returned his dissertation with the complaint that it was too short. Einstein said he added one more sentence, whereupon the paper was immediately accepted.

Finally Albert was Dr. Einstein.

Eleven days after finishing the dissertation, he mailed off his second revolutionary paper. As he summarized it, "The second paper is a determination of the true sizes of atoms." The question was still being argued as to whether all matter really was composed of small particles called atoms, joined together to form molecules. A couple of important scientists were still unsure. Yes, there was much theoretical evidence for the existence of atoms, but no direct physical proof. Atoms were so tiny that even with the strongest microscope, no one had ever seen one.

It had been observed that small particles such as dust motes and grains of pollen jiggle randomly when suspended in water. Why? No one knew, but the phenomenon had a name: Brownian motion, after the Scottish botanist Robert Brown, who had first described it in 1828. He thought the particles might somehow be alive. In 1865, a group of scientists had examined particles jumping around for *a whole year*—and the dancing had never stopped. Maybe electricity was involved.

Einstein believed that Brownian motion was caused by random collisions. Water molecules were bumping into the pollen grains. Other scientists had dismissed this idea because water molecules were so tiny. How could they move the much bigger pollen grains? But Einstein said, maybe one water molecule was insufficient to move a grain of pollen. But what about the combination of millions of collisions? He was able to work out the equations that showed exactly how far all these collisions would make a particle move in a given time. (The same method can be used to predict the result of all kinds of random motion, even the zigzag walk of a person who's had too much alcohol to drink.)

In his paper, Einstein made precise predictions that could be tested experimentally. And as usual, he ended by asking others to carry out the experiments. That took a while. Three years later, French physicist J. B. Perrin did so and confirmed Einstein's equations.

It was Perrin who ended up winning the Nobel Prize in 1926 for proving that atoms exist.

CHAPTER SIX

The Theory of Relativity
Plus the Famous Equation

*T*WO DAYS AFTER sending in his breathtaking Brownian paper, Einstein was brainstorming with Besso. They talked about the question Einstein had been asking himself since he was young: What would you experience if you were sitting on a beam of light as it traveled through space, or running along behind it at the speed of light? Einstein was frustrated. He had begun to worry that the laws of motion as laid out by Isaac Newton were not compatible with some of the new discoveries being made in physics.

One of Einstein's idols was James Clerk Maxwell

(he died the same year Einstein was born). Einstein always saw his goal as building upon the work of Maxwell, who took everything known about electricity, magnetism, and light and rolled it all into one unified theory—the electromagnetic theory. He came up with equations that correctly described how electricity, magnetism, and light behaved. They were actually forms of the same thing.

But there was a puzzling thing about Maxwell's equations. They seemed to say that light always traveled at the same speed. Didn't this contradict Newton's laws of motion, which dealt with the ways speed changed under various circumstances? To follow Newton's laws, the speed of light would have to be variable. And Newton's laws were the foundation of modern physics. How could they be wrong?

After gabbing with his friend throughout the night, Einstein was struck with one of his amazing insights while riding the streetcar home from Besso's house. Einstein was looking back at the famous Berne clock tower. He began to wonder what he would see if he were traveling away from the clock at the speed of light. He decided that since light from the clock face would never be able to catch up with him, it would

look to him as though the clock was frozen in a single, unchanging instant. If he carried a watch with him, however, it too would be moving at the speed of light and so would seem to him to keep telling time normally. This insight gave Einstein the key he needed for his next paper. Five weeks later, it was ready.

The third paper became the most famous. He was not boasting when he called the paper "a modification of the theory of space and time." Einstein realized that the key was thinking about "frames of reference." An observer's frame of reference changes according to his point of view. What happens is relative to who is observing. To an observer at the clock tower, Einstein would be racing at the speed of light. But from the point of view of the watch in his pocket, Einstein would not be moving at all.

This was not a new idea—Galileo had discussed the principle of relativity in 1639, and it had been accepted for day-to-day use ever since. But scientists thought that, beyond it, there must also be a more fundamental kind of "absolute" time and space that was always constant. Intuitively, it just felt right. Einstein was realizing that for the kinds of questions he wanted to answer, he couldn't assume these absolutes.

Imagine you're on a very long train that is traveling at ten miles per hour. You are walking down the aisle of the train at two miles per hour. From the point of view of someone sitting on the train watching you walk, you are moving at two miles per hour. But for someone outside, watching the train go by, you will have moved twelve miles in an hour—the ten miles the train traveled plus the two miles you walked. So for the observer, you are moving at twelve miles per hour.

But that's not all.

The earth is moving around the sun at 67,000 miles per hour, so for an observer on the sun, in an hour you have moved 67,012 miles. You are traveling at 67,012 miles per hour. So, how fast are you really moving? Einstein realized that there is no one ultimate right answer. Each is correct depending on your frame of reference.

As he continued to think about his light questions, Einstein made the first important assumption that led to his theory of special relativity: The laws of physics are always true, in any frame of reference. They don't change when the frame of reference changes—otherwise, they wouldn't be laws. So for instance, we know that distance equals rate multiplied by time. That just means if you travel at three miles per hour (your rate) for two hours (your time) your distance will be six miles. In the train example above, this holds true, no matter the frame of reference. Someone sitting on the train feels he hasn't covered any distance at all. An hour later he's still in the very same seat, at the same place. So, within the train, the distance he's traveled (zero miles) equals the rate at which he's been moving (zero miles per hour) times the time (one hour). But from the point of view of the observer outside the train, the passenger is now ten miles away, because the train has been moving at ten miles an hour. Again, distance (ten miles) equals rate (ten miles per hour) multiplied by time (one hour). And so on.

This is no problem at the kind of speeds we're used to observing. But what about something that moves as fast as light? Einstein thought about that some more. He took into account Maxwell's work, the way his equations always used the same, unchanging number for the speed of an electromagnetic wave in any of its forms, including light. Einstein also thought about the experimental work that two scientists—Albert Michelson and Edward Morley—had carried out in the late 1880s that showed that the speed of light didn't change no matter what direction it was coming from. What Einstein was able to understand was both grand and simple: The speed of light is a constant.

Frame of reference makes no difference. The speed of light never changes.

Now imagine the train again. One person is sitting on the train. A second person is waiting beside the tracks. This train is moving really, really fast—at one-half the speed of light. As the train passes, at the exact moment that the two people are side-by-side, the person in the train shines a flashlight toward the front end of the car, 100 feet ahead of him. Think about the instant that beam of light hits the front wall of the car. From the point of view of the passenger, the light has traveled 100 feet. But from the point of view of the person outside, by the time the light reaches the wall, the train has traveled 50 feet farther, so the light beam has traveled 150 feet.

Now, according to Einstein, the laws of physics can't change. For both the passenger and the person outside, distance always equals rate multiplied by time. But for the two observers the distance is different. How is this possible? Is the speed of the flashlight beam different for the two frames of reference? No, it can't be, because the speed of light is constant. So then it must be time that is different for the two observers. For the passenger, less time has passed than for the person on the ground.

Of course, common sense says this conclusion is silly. But Einstein persisted despite running up against common sense. He followed through on his idea, figuring out what this new way of thinking about time and space would mean for all kinds of scientific questions, and he discovered, strange as it seemed, that it gave him many answers that made sense in ways no other theory could. If Einstein was right, space and time were connected to each other and affected each other. In a way they were forms of the same thing. It could lead to situations that even now sound like science fiction—if someone travels to outer space and back fast enough, on his return he will be younger than his identical twin who stayed on Earth. (Time would have moved faster for the twin on Earth.)

To come up with his theory of relativity, Einstein left out certain factors, the most important being the force of gravity. He did this to make his answers as uncomplicated and clear as possible. That is why today we call his theory "special." It applies only under special circumstances.

As a joke, since no one understood relativity anyway, he once gave this picture: "Put your hand on a hot stove for a minute, and it seems like a hour. Sit with a pretty girl for an hour, and it seems like a minute. That's relativity."

Among other results of his theory that would affect the rest of the century, Einstein finally, at age twenty-six, had the answer to his confounding question as a sixteen-year-old.

Q: What would it be like riding a beam of light?

A: Time would stand still.

After nearly killing himself with this third paper, he took to his bed, exhausted, for two weeks. The story is that Mileva combed through the article over and over, fixing mistakes, before mailing it off. Then the two went out for an uncharacteristically wild celebration.

Almost as an afterthought to the last paper, he scribbled three more pages. These became the final paper of his miracle year. It dealt with two basic building blocks of the scientific world—mass (the amount of matter in an object) and energy. He theorized that they were really two different forms of the same thing and could be converted into each other. He created an equation, possibly the most famous equation of all time. $E = mc^2$. In the equation, E stands for energy, m is mass, and c is the speed of light. "Squared" means that c is multiplied by itself. The equation tells us that a very tiny amount of mass is the equivalent of an incredibly large amount of energy.

Einstein's equation solved many problems that had

been puzzling scientists. For instance, Marie Curie had recently been working with newly discovered radioactive substances, metals that seemed to emit a stream of energy without ever getting any smaller. How? And how was it possible for the sun and other stars to give off huge amounts of energy without burning out? The answer was that stars as well as radioactive elements were converting the mass of individual atoms into energy . . . a frightening thought if it became possible for people to use the same kind of process to release the enormous amount of energy present in a chain of split atoms.

Reverberations of Einstein's equation continue to the present day.

Whew. Einstein's socalled miracle year, 1905, remains almost impossible to fathom. In one creative burst, he came up with a quantum theory of light, gave decisive proof for the existence of atoms, explained Brownian motion, and altered our notions of space and time, matter, and energy. One of the many astonishing aspects of his genius was his ability to think about all these problems simultaneously. Later he said the key to his miracle year was remaining a child, asking the simplest of questions.

In several letters to Mileva, Einstein referred to "our theory." Ever since, debate has raged about how much credit she deserves. Was she actually the co-founder of the theory of relativity, ignored because of prejudice against women in science?

Mileva *was* among the few who understood what he was doing, someone he could bounce ideas off. She clearly did some of the research, and as always helped him with math—"She solves all the mathematical problems for me," Einstein stated. But there is no evidence she did more than that.

We actually don't know much about his private thoughts during this crucial year. He used only Besso and Mileva as sounding boards, and not one of the three kept a diary. Einstein included no footnotes in his papers and later credited only his lofty conversations with Besso in developing his theories. He kept his notes in baby Hans's carriage and took them out during strolls with the child up and down the lovely streets of Berne.

He didn't have clear ideas about how the theories would be put to use—that was for others to figure out. That's why he ended each of the papers with a call to others to test his theories, to react, to talk back to him.

Feedback—that's what Einstein was waiting for.

CHAPTER SEVEN

Junior Professor, with Hair

S O? WHAT WAS the reaction to the young genius's four papers? Most of the physics community ignored them. Scientists who bothered to react had sharp criticisms. With anti-Semitism on the rise, some arbitrarily labeled his science "too Jewish" and "unhealthy" in its lack of respect for Newton's laws. Others complained that Einstein's work was too abstract. His theories contradicted most of what physics professors were teaching and went against information we get from our five senses. There was also general disbelief—how could he have come up with all this? He didn't even have a lab—where were his data? Who was this guy? A clerk . . . where?

Einstein snared the attention of just one physicist—but it was none other than Max Planck, the best possible fan Einstein could have. As the founder of quantum theory, Planck was the most influential physicist of his generation. Planck published an article in 1906 praising Einstein's work. He wrote to Einstein requesting to meet him the next year. Meanwhile, he sent his assistant to the Berne patent office. So humble a figure did the patent clerk cut that the assistant first walked right by Einstein, never imagining this young man could be the fabled genius.

Planck's encouragement went a long way. In between clerking, playing violin in a string quartet once a week, and amusing Hans, Einstein published six more papers in 1906 and ten more the following year.

Before most people had even read his relativity theory, he was already spotting its limitations and continuing to tweak it. There seemed to be two crucial things missing: It made no mention of either gravitation or acceleration. He craved an even broader theory, something more unifying, more general than what he had so far.

According to legend, he was sitting in his office in 1907 when he saw a painter fall off the roof nearby.

Einstein suddenly had this thought: "If a person falls freely, he will not feel his own weight." Did this actually happen? Who knows?

Was it possible that Newton's gravitational force was actually a by-product of something else, something deeper? Could gravity be related to motion? Here was a new way of looking at Newton's gravity—as acceleration. Einstein later termed this "the happiest thought in my life." It jump-started his attempt to *generalize* his *special* theory of relativity and make it apply to all situations; he realized he could incorporate the idea of accelerated motion. Not that the solution was quick— sustained by his vision, hindered by his math skills, he would not come up with a general theory for eight more years.

Years that were apparently going to be spent clerking at the patent office. Earning his PhD did get him a promotion at work, from third-class to second-class expert, with a nice raise. But still no job offers came from any university. "History is full of bad jokes," one friend sympathized.

Rebelliousness continued to work against him in academic circles. Einstein did himself no favors. In applying for one academic post, he was asked how he kept up with current scientific research. He said he didn't, offering the lame excuse, "The library is closed in my free time." In 1907, in order to become a lowly lecturer at the University of Berne, Einstein submitted seventeen of his published papers. But when the university demanded one more paper, something that hadn't been published yet, he stubbornly refused—and didn't get the job.

He started checking out jobs at high schools, also with no luck. Of twenty-one applicants for a math teacher position, he didn't make the final cut of three. Finally he swallowed his pride and wrote the required new paper for the University of Berne and became a lecturer. Yet the pay was so low that he couldn't quit the patent office. Now he was working two jobs.

Like his fellow genius Newton, Einstein wasn't a natural-born teacher. His lectures were poorly attended, sometimes by only one listener. He was disorganized, sometimes ill-prepared (which he freely admitted), disconnected from his audience. One of his rivals wrote he "had no understanding how to relate to people." His looks didn't help—his pants usually too short, his hair sprouting in every direction.

Not until 1909—*nine years* after graduating from Polytechnic—was he offered a satisfactory academic job. After Einstein delivered a well-prepared, well-received lecture at the University of Zürich on relativity, his old thesis adviser, Alfred Kleiner, recommended him for a newly created professorship in theoretical physics. The salary at the University of Zürich was low. Many on the faculty thought Einstein was "too Jewish." And the offer came with a warning: Einstein had to be open to advice about improving his teaching.

He accepted, but only after the starting salary was raised. At age thirty, he was now a junior professor at the University of Zürich.

Einstein never became a great teacher, but he was motivated to get better. Using small strips of paper with scribbled notes, he lectured in what was actually a useful way, showing the step-by-step development of his ideas. How amazing for students to hear Einstein explain how Einstein's mind worked! He allowed interruptions and questions (rare among professors then), and he would gather students around for an informal chat, maybe grabbing one by the arm to stress a point. Demonstrating how he could work on two problems at the same time, he would ask for help with "some silly mathematical transformation that I can't find for a moment," go on talking about something entirely different and then, minutes later, burst forth with the solution to the math problem himself.

After class he might invite students to the Café
Terasse or to his house for coffee. Always he enjoyed
strong coffee, cigars, and a good joke. (Later in life one
of his favorite books was *The Hundred Best Jewish Jokes*.)
His own laugh, which sounded like a seal barking, was
contagious.

In his second year, he was asked to supervise lab
work. Horrors! He was the first to admit his reluctance
to "pick up a piece of apparatus for fear it might blow
up." Yet his students, worried that other job offers
would be coming his way, put together a petition to
keep Einstein in Zürich, calling his lectures "a great
delight."

It seemed that Albert Einstein was finally on a
roll. In 1911 he was appointed a full professor at the
University of Prague, more prestigious than Zürich
and at twice the pay. He got the job despite initially
messing up the application form. He wrote "none" in
the space for "religion." It was a truthful reflection
of his beliefs. Except for a brief period when he was
about nine, he had always rebelled against organized religion. But having no religion was even more offensive
than being Jewish (which in many places was plenty
offensive enough). So to land the job he finally listed

himself as "Mosaic"—a follower of the prophet Moses.

Once settled in Prague, the Einsteins had a cushier life. They had electric lights for the first time, plus a live-in maid. Einstein's office overlooked a park that was part of an insane asylum—he said he felt a kinship with the inmates he'd see on their daily walks. He hung out at fancy parties with the intellectual elite, including writer Franz Kafka.

But Mileva was worried: "I only hope that fame does not exert a detrimental influence on his human side." The higher he soared, the more it became apparent that as a family man he made a great scientist. With his second son, Eduard, born in 1910, he wasn't spending the same quality time that he had with Hans.

His relationship with Mileva was curdling. She was jealous of his new friends—women and men—and jealous of his new success. "With that kind of fame, he does not have much time for his wife," she wrote in one bitter letter. To visitors she sometimes seemed severely depressed, sitting in a corner and not speaking. Einstein was not only unsympathetic but irritated. He also worried about Eduard, who was having trouble eating and sleeping, and he feared the boy might not survive to adulthood.

"Worries and more worries," he wrote to a friend, adding, "Nevertheless, I have found a nice generalization of the Sommerfeld-Epstein quantum law." As always, thinking about science was his escape, his joy. . . .

So was spending time with colleagues. He finally met some of the heroes he'd studied in college, such as Dutch physicist Hendrik Lorentz, who became almost a father figure to Einstein. "I admire this man like no other; I might say, I love him," said Einstein. He paid regular visits to Lorentz's house, where he was offered the most comfortable chair, given a cigar, and urged to talk, talk, talk. Einstein said Lorentz "meant more to me personally than anybody else I have met in my lifetime."

He was surrounded by admiring peers at the first Solvay Conference in 1911 in Brussels. This important science conference was by invitation only, and he was the baby, at thirty-two, among heavyweights like Marie Curie, Poincaré, and Planck. The topic was quantum theory—how to reconcile it with classic Newtonian physics. Einstein privately thought some of the scientists "showed little grasp" of quantum theory. He dismissed his own talk ("The Present State of the Problem of Specific Heats") as "twaddle."

Just as the conference was starting, Marie Curie received word that she'd won her second Nobel Prize. Curie *did* impress Einstein. He respected her "sparkling intelligence," and the two were to cross paths several times in the coming years. One summer vacation, his family and hers went hiking together in the Alps, Einstein talking nonstop to Curie about passengers in a falling elevator, gravity, acceleration.

Marie Curie was "not attractive enough," in Einstein's words, to ever be more than a friend. But another woman did charm him. He became reacquainted with someone from his childhood—Elsa Einstein (a first cousin on his mother's side and a second cousin on his father's side). Elsa wrote from Berlin to ask which book on relativity she should read, and he boldly offered to explain his theory in person. They began an affair. She was three years older, divorced with two daughters, an excellent cook, and nurturing—one of her first presents to him was a hairbrush. Einstein, who disliked confrontation, saw no need to push Mileva for a divorce. (He so avoided conflict of any kind that he didn't even like to play chess, bridge, or the new game of Monopoly.)

Then, in 1912, with a crucial letter of recommendation from Marie Curie, Einstein was at long last offered a post at his alma mater. Polytechnic was now a full university, the Swiss Federal Institute of Technology. He wrote a postcard to friends declaring, "Great joy about it among us old folks and the two bear cubs." Even better, his old note-taking pal, Grossmann, was now professor of geometry and chairman of the math department.

The Einsteins took a beautiful, six-room apartment with views, where they hosted musical gatherings. But Mileva developed disabling rheumatism and became even more of a burden to her husband. The couple argued frequently about their children and finances. She was jealous, doubtless suspecting his affair. She nagged. Again, Einstein's strategy was avoidance. He spent more and more time on the road, speaking at international conferences or locking himself up at home alone and losing himself in contemplating how to generalize his theory of relativity. It was frustrating work. In desperation, he would drop by his old pal's office after lunch: "Grossmann, you've got to help me or I will go crazy."

His frustration, however, would soon give way to another beautiful, brilliant breakthrough.

CHAPTER EIGHT

Too Beautiful to Be False

*T*HE ACADEMIC TIDE had turned in favor of Einstein.

A tempting triple-offer came from the University of Berlin, thanks to Planck and others. Besides a professorship, the German offer promised his election to the Prussian Academy of Sciences (whose fifty members—all men—pompously addressed one another as "Your Excellency"). He'd be its youngest member at age thirty-four. He would also become the director of a new research center, the Kaiser Wilhelm Institute for Physics . . . and the salary was hefty, with no teaching required—too good to be true.

To accept meant leaving Switzerland again and hiding his contempt for all things German. But he would be in the same city as Cousin Elsa and her home cooking. Einstein teased Planck by delaying his response, saying if he waved a red rose from the train station, it meant he accepted. A white rose meant no go.

A red rose it was. It was 1913 and he was poised at the height of his academic career.

As his new life began in Berlin, his marriage was in its death throes. "I treat my wife as an employee whom I cannot fire," he wrote to a friend. A bizarre and cruel letter to Mileva proposed a contract in which she was to make sure "that my clothes and laundry are kept in good order, that I will receive my three meals regularly *in my room*." He went on, "You will not expect any intimacy from me . . . you will stop talking to me if I request it." In return he offered only to continue living with her and act with the politeness "such as I would exercise to any woman as a stranger."

Oddly enough, she accepted the deal. But shortly afterward, she reneged. Mileva took custody of the boys and got on the train back to Zürich.

After seeing them off, Einstein did something very surprising, something he hardly ever did: He cried, mourning the loss of his sons. He planned to keep up a relationship with them, but swore he'd never marry again—it was just too "confining."

Living alone, he decided, was "an indescribable blessing." (Not entirely alone, as Elsa and her two daughters, Margot and Ilse, lived conveniently nearby.) He worked as many hours as he liked, slept when he pleased, and if he remembered to eat at all, would heat whatever was around in a saucepan.

He avoided the work he'd been hired to do—staffing his new Institute for Physics, which was created to do further research on quantum theory.

Instead, he kept to himself, obsessing over how to generalize his special theory of relativity. Two steps forward, one step back—he made progress, found mistakes and corrected them, and continued to wage war with math, consulting with Grossmann long-distance. "I have gained enormous respect for mathematics," he said at one point.

Previously, Einstein had thrown out the well-entrenched Newtonian concept of absolute time. Time is relative, Einstein had theorized.

Now he looked at Newton's concept of space, in which "absolute space, in its own nature, without relation to anything external, remains always similar and immovable." Einstein threw this out too: Space is relative as well. Space *and* time are dependent upon the frame of reference.

In fact, space and time are *fused* in a way he visualized as a fabric. A fabric that curves and bends. A four-dimensional fabric that constitutes our universe.

How can this be true? It seems so counterintuitive to reality as we perceive it. But this curvature of space-time is something we're not even aware of. As Einstein described it, "When a blind beetle crawls over the surface of a curved branch, it doesn't notice that the path it has covered is indeed curved." What we—or blind beetles–don't notice, Einstein did. And what he was trying to do was quantify it and prove it.

In Einstein's new world, gravity is not a force, as Newton said, but is actually a by-product of the bending of the fabric of space and time, created by the presence of a mass. Gravity was a *warping* of space and time. Space and time *curve* to form the ripples we know as gravity.

None of this is easy for ordinary mortals to understand. But try this thought experiment. Picture a bowling ball rolling onto a trampoline—can you see the curve in the rubbery surface of the trampoline as the bowling ball pulls it down? Now roll some marbles onto the trampoline. The marbles will roll toward the bowling ball. The gravity in space-time works something like this: The marbles don't move toward the bowling ball because the ball is pulling them. They're just following the path of the rubber trampoline surface. In the same way, an apple doesn't fall toward the earth because gravity is pulling it with some mysterious magnetic force. The mass of the earth has curved the fabric of space-time around it, so that the apple's natural path is toward the earth.

All forms of motion, Einstein deduced, can be explained by the curves in this fabric of space-time.

The implications were enormous. For example, from Einstein's theory, one could deduce that gravity bent light. In other words, even light would always follow the curve of space-time.

If light really did bend when it passed near the sun, then a solar eclipse could become crucial. During a solar eclipse, which hides light from the sun, astronomers would be able to observe the light from distant stars. If Einstein's theory was correct, the light would bend as it passed the sun. This would make it seem to the observers as if the star was in a different place from where it really was. Einstein's theory predicted how much this deflection of light by the sun should be.

Normally bored by experiments, he couldn't wait for August 12, 1914, when a total eclipse of the sun would present the perfect opportunity to prove him right. The best spot for an astronomer to take measure-ments was determined to be the Crimea, in what was then the Russian Empire; soon plans were under way for an expedition there. Einstein was so excited, he even offered to help fund the trip. Private donations made that unnecessary.

Alas, world events got in the way. On June 28, 1914, World War I—a.k.a. the Great War and the War to End All Wars—broke out. It quickly grew into a cataclysmic global conflict.

Only twenty days before the eclipse, with an as-tronomer already en route to the Crimea, Germany de-clared war on Russia. To the Russian Army, Einstein's astronomer, with his telescopes and cameras, looked more like a spy than a scientist. He was arrested, and although he was released a few weeks later, the eclipse had come and gone. No experiment.

The missed opportunity was not a bad thing,

Einstein was to find out later. He had made miscalculations, and the experiment, with a lot of attendant embarrassing publicity, would in fact have proven him wrong.

His ego unbruised, Einstein kept working on his own, gaining momentum even without the necessary proof. His equations for general relativity had flaws he couldn't seem to get around, and he was beginning to realize that some needed to be reworked.

In the summer of 1915, even with some equations still unfinished, he felt solid enough to present several lectures that laid out his theory of general relativity. In the audience was a German mathematician, David Hilbert. He saw at once what Einstein was up to. Hilbert was grappling with the very same equations as Einstein. They became friends, but they were also competitors. In fact, Hilbert could see the flaws in Einstein's equations and wanted to solve them first. A race was on.

Day after day, Einstein kept pounding away, running into roadblocks. For every problem solved, new ones arose.

November of 1915 saw his stress level soar; stomach pains were starting to plague him. On successive Thursdays, Einstein planned a series of four lectures to the Prussian Academy. Even as he began the first,

he was still working frantically on the other three. He was all too aware that Hilbert was nipping at his heels. Einstein was determined to get the equations first, no matter how many late nights he had to put in. The question of priority—who gets there first—is an important one, not just for the scientist's ego, but for the history of science.

During the delivery of his lectures, Einstein was like someone balancing on a high wire, so exhilarated that his heart palpitated. He traced the complete history of his thought process, honestly admitting his mistakes and difficulties. In the last lecture, on November 25, he triumphantly presented complete mathematical equations that represented his general theory of relativity.

The equations were amazingly complicated—nothing as short and catchy as $E = mc^2$. Only other genius physicists could attempt to grasp them.

Another solar eclipse was due in four years. "It would be a most desirable thing if astronomers would take up the question," Einstein concluded humbly.

And what about David Hilbert? Five days *before* Einstein's final lecture, Hilbert submitted a paper to a scientific journal. It may have contained his own equations for general relativity. (Or they may have been added at a later date.) The stage was set for a battle over priority. Science historians continue to debate this, but in the end Hilbert himself gave Einstein priority and full credit. The two were even able to remain friends. Today the equations are known as "the Einstein-Hilbert action," but the theory itself is attributed solely to Einstein.

Einstein had copies of the four speeches sent to all his friends, attaching comments such as "The theory is of incomparable beauty." Giddy with confidence, he felt his new general theory of relativity was simply too beautiful—mathematically speaking—to be false.

At age thirty-six, Einstein was incredibly proud—and limp with exhaustion.

CHAPTER NINE

Stomach Pain

*T*HE BIG BREAKTHROUGH took its toll. Einstein lost weight, fifty pounds in all. Although he claimed half-jokingly that he didn't mind dying now that he'd finished his theory, he was in great pain. (The stomach trouble that had been hounding him grew worse and continued for the rest of his life.) Doctors put him on a restricted diet of macaroni, rice, and zwieback bread.

There wasn't much to do except try to relax, savor his moment, and wait for acclaim. He spent a year writing a book for the general public called *Relativity: The Special and the General Theory.* As he wrote, he read every page aloud to Elsa's daughter Margot, to make sure he could explain things to an ordinary person. She politely assured him she understood everything, later revealing to others she was in fact clueless.

The global conflict dragged on, with an ultimate death toll of an estimated twenty million people. In wartime Germany, food was proving harder and harder to get, and the shortages didn't help Einstein's stomach. Resourceful Elsa somehow found eggs and butter, as well as the impossible-to-get cigars he loved. Slowly he started gaining weight back.

During a vacation at the seashore, he tried to rest and retreat from the war, writing that he didn't "give a hoot about the so-called world." When out in the sun, he would make hats out of his handkerchief—a flat surface altered with knots to become a curved surface, which he couldn't help noticing was like the fabric of space-time. . . .

And he did give a hoot about the world. While some scientists were helping their governments by devising new ways to kill, Einstein believed strongly that scientists had a particular duty to *stop* wars. A dedicated pacifist, he had been only one of four intellectuals in Germany to sign a manifesto opposing that country's entry into war. Disgusted, he called nationalism "the measles of mankind." He would write, "At such a time as this, one realizes what a sorry species of animal one belongs to."

Oddly enough, it was his stance on the war (rather than his scientific achievements) that brought Einstein to the attention of the public at large. And recognition from within the scientific community was growing as well— experiments that confirmed his theories, and an animated silent film about the theory of relativity in 1919.

That year, under pressure from Elsa, he finally persuaded Mileva to formally end their marriage. He'd been offering better and better terms for a divorce, eventually promising her the money from a Nobel Prize, if he ever won one. The promise may seem obnoxiously over-confident, but by then he had already been nominated—and passed over—six times. Mileva spent several days mulling over this offer, but in the end she accepted. "I do not want to stand in the way of your happiness."

His sons, Hans and Eduard, were fifteen and nine at the time. In the years that followed, he and Mileva were both models of bad post-divorce behavior, each trying to turn their sons against the other parent.

Never a particularly close father, Einstein did keep up a relationship with his sons. When he was with Hans and Eduard they played music, went sailing, built model airplanes. He even fantasized about home-schooling them himself: "You can learn a lot of good things from me that no one else can offer you." That undoubtedly was true, but he was not cut out for full-time parenting. He enjoyed his sons as long as they were "clever" and "undemanding," but grew impatient when they misbehaved. Then Einstein could turn childish himself—petty, defensive.

The domestic turmoil never distracted Einstein from the focus of his life: "The love of science thrives under these circumstances, for it lifts me impersonally from the vale of tears into peaceful spheres." Unlike science, reality was all "painful crudity and hopeless dreariness," without "peace and security." With sadness—and with honesty—Einstein admitted, "I have *not* bestowed the same care to understanding people as to understanding science." He called himself a "lone traveler" without strong attachment to a country, community, friends, even family.

Five months after his divorce, however, he married Cousin Elsa. Elsa didn't understand relativity—and didn't want to. "Although she may get on my nerves at times and is no mental brainstorm," Einstein later told Hans, "she is exceptionally kindhearted." His new wife was a proper Hausfrau: "My interest in mathematics is mainly in the household bills," she said. They had separate bedrooms in a large apartment, respectably furnished (her taste, not his) with a large study for him in the attic. He worked in a comfortable armchair with a pad of paper, surrounded by clouds of blue smoke and piles of paper. She wasn't allowed to enter without permission, and he could be unpleasant if she did.

Elsa called him "the professor" and treated him like the classic absentminded genius he was by packing his suitcases, doling out spending money, keeping away distractions. She would call him down from his study for meals and not mind if there was no conversation. She prepared his favorite comfort foods, such as lentil soup with sausages, egg-drop soup, salmon with mayonnaise, strawberries with whipped cream. He drank huge quantities of black tea, and he loved honey so much that they bought it in buckets. Sometimes he would follow a meal by asking her or a daughter to go for a walk. It was understood they had to wait to be asked; they couldn't simply join him.

Up until 1919 there were more no-votes than yes-votes for Einstein's revolutionary theories. Relativity was considered by some to be far out of the mainstream of scientific thought, counterintuitive, disorienting. Some even feared that it referred to ethics and human behavior, that "everything is relative" translated into "anything goes." Einstein always took care to point out his relativity applied to measurements of time and space, not morals. (He hadn't even wanted to call it "theory of relativity"—other physicists came up with this and the name stuck.)

Then, on May 29, 1919, came another solar eclipse, when photographs could be taken that offered a chance to prove Einstein's theory of general relativity. The war, which had begun just before the previous eclipse, ended just before this one. During the war, England and Germany had been enemies. Now English scientists were working toward proving a German theory; one team set out for an island off the coast of West Africa to see the eclipse, and in case clouds obscured the view there, another team headed to a town in the Amazon jungle of northern Brazil. In a way, Einstein the pacifist was bringing about postwar cooperation.

The weather was cloudy, but for five minutes the

sky cleared—enough time for numerous photographs to be taken. But results were not instant. The technology of photography was far from what it is today. All the photographic plates had to be shipped back to England, developed, measured—and not for four months did the world know the results.

They confirmed Einstein's theory. Light indeed bent as it passed near the sun. We live in a curved universe.

He got the news in a telegram on September 22. At the time, he was with a student who said he showed her the telegram and beamed. "I *knew* the theory was correct," he said. She asked what if the results had shown otherwise. He answered, "Then I would have been sorry for the dear Lord; the theory is correct."

Later, with more modesty, he wrote, "Newton, forgive me." Then he went out to buy himself a new violin to celebrate.

In November, the news was announced publicly in London at a joint meeting of the Royal Society and the Royal Astronomical Society. Nobel laureate J. J. Thomson declared, "This result is not an isolated one, it is a whole continent of scientific ideas. . . . This is the most important result obtained in connection with the theory of gravitation since Newton's day . . . one of the greatest achievements of human thought."

Newspaper headlines in London screamed: "Revolution in Science—New Theory of the Universe—Newtonian Ideas Overthrown—Momentous Pronouncement—Space 'Warped.'" In New York headlines echoed: "Men of Science More or Less Agog over Results of Eclipse Observations . . . EINSTEIN THEORY TRIUMPHS . . . Stars Not Where They Seemed or Were Calculated to Be, but Nobody Need Worry."

At age forty, Albert Einstein was the most famous scientist on the planet. He had eclipsed Isaac Newton.

CHAPTER TEN

Fame

*A*LL SPOTLIGHTS WERE trained on Einstein. He was a celebrity scientist. In the first six years after the 1919 eclipse, more than six hundred articles and books about relativity appeared. His own primer became an unlikely bestseller that the public tried, without much luck, to understand.

He was hounded by reporters. Magazines such as *Time* and *Life* were just starting to take off, as were radio and newsreels in movie theaters. Einstein thought most stories about him were "drivel." Like Curie, whose fame made her publicity-shy, he complained about "riffraff" seeking him out—"It's so dreadful I can barely breathe anymore, not to mention getting around to any sensible work." Unlike Curie, he had real difficulty saying no to requests for interviews.

In fact, his attitude toward publicity was clearly ambivalent. At first he was squeamish about press conferences—"like undressing in public." But soon he was mugging for the cameras. Elsa encouraged this public persona, more certain about fame—she liked it, and she started charging money for his autographs and photographs, donating the money to charity.

As he gave more interviews, Einstein mastered the art of the clever sound bite. "I've just developed a new theory of eternity," he quipped during a night of long, boring speeches. He became such a witty speaker that there are whole books of Einstein quotes.

The most frequent request from reporters was for a one-sentence explanation of the theory of relativity. Ha! Instead of laughing hysterically, he protested that it would take from three to four hours just to give the basics. The closest he ever came was this: "It is a theory of space and time as far as physics is concerned, which leads to a theory of gravitation."

No reporter had the slightest idea what he was talking about, but it almost didn't matter. Einstein made great copy. After the destruction and horror of World War I, his brilliance, the beauty of his abstract thought, seemed a sign of human potential for good. His retorts, his marvelous brain, his kindly smile, and that cloud of wiry hair (cartoonists loved him)—he was adorable. He won even more fans whenever he played his violin instead of giving a speech.

A few scientists were already warning him that $E = mc^2$ could pave the way to the production of "frightening explosives." Einstein pooh-poohed the very idea.

He was more worried about conditions in postwar Germany, which were going from bad to terrible. Six million German soldiers had been killed in the war. The defeated empire suffered under the harsh terms of surrender. In the new, frail, democratic Germany, unemployment was rampant, food was scarce, and prices for everyday items skyrocketed. From 1919 to 1920 the value of the German mark sank so low that a loaf of bread became unaffordable. People carted wheelbarrows of money to buy basic goods.

Einstein saw the future. "People need a scapegoat and make the Jews responsible," he wrote in 1920. That held true even in science. Increasingly vocal anti-Semites labeled his theory "Jewish physics" and called him a self-promoter trying to make a business out of science. One group of German scientists ridiculed his theory as a hoax.

The fiercest attacks came from German physicist Philipp Lenard, a former influence on Einstein, someone he'd once admired. Lenard told Einstein to his face that the theory of relativity "offends against the simple common sense of a scientist." A few months after this encounter, a then-unknown German politician named Adolf Hitler wrote, "Science, once our greatest pride, is today being taught by Hebrews."

Interestingly, as anti-Semitism grew more overt, Einstein came to a much greater appreciation of his Jewish identity. He never attended a synagogue, but he declared, "My relationship to the Jewish people has become my strongest human tie." He supported early efforts to create a Jewish homeland in Palestine, while expressing concern for Palestinians being displaced. On his first trip to the United States, in 1921, he used his celebrity to raise money for the new settlements. (Not until 1948—after World War II and the Nazi annihilation of six million Jews—was the state of Israel born.)

In June 1922, the assassination of a prominent Jewish politician and friend shook Einstein to the core.

Police warned him that his name was on a hit list as well. "I am always on the alert," he wrote. He told Marie Curie he was prepared to leave Berlin (she thought he should stay and fight back), but he made no move to pack up. He had lived in the city eight years, longer than anywhere else, and he led a comfortable life. He tried to take the long view, that Earth's problems were small: "This is a very small star, and probably some of the larger and more important stars may be very virtuous and happy."

So in Berlin he remained. He was supposed to be running the Institute of Physics. It's an understatement to say Einstein wasn't a good administrator. He accomplished little aside from hiring one astronomer and bringing in his stepdaughter Ilse to do secretarial work.

For a brief moment he thought about abandoning science and working as an engineer in a quiet, "normal human existence," with lots of time for sailing, his favorite hobby. The thought passed.

He accepted invitations to speak around the world. Everywhere, thousands greeted him, treating him like a rock star with parades, flowers, keys to cities. In the United States, the Senate put the theory of relativity on its list of topics to debate during the 1921 session of Congress. While being photographed with Einstein, President Warren Harding had to admit that he for one didn't get it. At Princeton University in New Jersey, Einstein received an honorary degree for "voyaging through strange seas of thought." His lectures there lasted four hours, during which he wrote more than 125 math equations on the blackboard.

What about his Nobel Prize? The Nobel committee had been passing him over since 1910. They liked to reward scientists whose work included precise data accumulated from laborious experiments, and Einstein, who said things like "Imagination is more important than knowledge," didn't exactly fit the mold. There was also jealousy over his superstar status, as well as opposition from anti-Semitic enemies. The absence of a prize was getting embarrassing—to him, of course, and also to the committee, who realized how ridiculous their refusal of recognition for Einstein looked.

Then, just as he was preparing for a trip to Japan in 1922, word came that he had been awarded the Nobel Prize for Physics. Ironically, the prize wasn't for relativity, still considered too theoretical and not grounded in experiments. The prize was for his work way back in 1905 on the law of the photoelectric effect.

The prize was a sum ten times more than a typical professor's annual salary, and it was paid in valuable Swedish currency, not worthless German marks. As he'd promised, the money went to Mileva and was ultimately used to pay for the care of their younger son, Eduard, who was developing emotional problems in addition to other ailments.

During his acceptance speech in Sweden, Einstein—ever the maverick—spoke about relativity instead of the photoelectric effect. He'd specifically been asked *not* to talk about it, but the king of Sweden, sitting in the front row, wanted to try to understand it.

On the way back to Germany, he stopped in Copenhagen to visit Niels Bohr, a Danish physicist six years his junior. Bohr was proving most influential in furthering the development of quantum mechanics, a scientific offshoot of quantum theory. Because quantum mechanics was starting to unravel secrets of atoms and molecules, it was absorbing the interest of the majority of younger physicists. They were not working on relativity. Even though his work had helped introduce quantum theory to the world, Einstein was unhappy with the way the idea was developing. He worried that scientists were going in the wrong direction.

Bohr and Einstein rode a streetcar together, talking so intensely that they passed the stop for Bohr's house. They turned around, then talked past their stop again. "We rode to and fro, and I can well imagine what the people thought about us," Bohr wrote.

Bohr became one of Einstein's favorite sparring partners. Einstein wrote him, "Not often in life has a human being caused me such joy by his mere presence as you did." For years they engaged in furious arguments over science. Bohr would get so worked up, he'd walk around the house afterward sputtering, "Einstein, Einstein, Einstein!"

What really agitated Einstein about quantum mechanics was that as it developed, it increasingly implied a fundamental randomness in the universe. Too much depended on chance. "Physics should represent a reality in time and space," Einstein always insisted, "free from spooky action at a distance." His most famous way of phrasing this was to say that "God does not play dice with the universe," meaning that there are no random events. He said this often; if Bohr was around, he would retort that Einstein should stop telling God what to do.

Although Einstein had claimed to have no religion,

he was not an atheist. As for the nature of God, Einstein said, "We are in the position of a little child entering a huge library filled with books in many languages. The child dimly suspects a mysterious order in the arrangement of the books but doesn't know what it is. That, it seems to me, is the attitude of even the most intelligent human being toward God."

Einstein stubbornly resisted the rise of quantum mechanics, which had the effect of isolating him from the rest of the physics community. He was off by himself, thinking, thinking, thinking. He hoped to pull together two thousand years of ideas about the universe into one very big idea.

A Theory of Everything.

CHAPTER ELEVEN

Escape to America

*B*Y 1925, EINSTEIN had become obsessed with discovering one all-embracing theory that would unify the forces of the universe and the laws of physics into a single, grand framework. Like Leonardo da Vinci more than five hundred years earlier, Einstein was thinking Big with a capital B—looking for a system for understanding *everything*.

Einstein was on the hunt for what was termed a unified field theory—one that would explain away the seemingly random quality of quantum mechanics that bothered him so much. Although the theory of general relativity worked and quantum theory worked, it was impossible to come up with an equation that included both theories. They were incompatible, and Einstein did not believe that the universe would be founded on two fundamentally incompatible things.

Most scientists, who were by then invested in pursuing quantum mechanics, did not think a unified field theory was possible. Einstein, on the other hand, thought it would *underlie* quantum theory as a whole.

Physics was moving so rapidly that he was becoming its cranky old man. When he was invited to the 1927 and 1930 Solvay Conferences, he showed up mainly to duel with the others, especially Niels Bohr, over the quantum problem. "Deep down it is wrong, even if it is empirically and logically right," Einstein declared. Breakfasts at Solvay were torture. He'd stay up all night trying to find logical inconsistencies in the theory of quantum mechanics, devising sophisticated new thought experiments, then bring them to breakfast. The other physicists would set to work and prove him wrong by dinnertime. This went on for days.

He continued to struggle with his theory of relativity. It seemed to indicate that the universe is dynamic—continually expanding or contracting. This was such a contradiction of the then-current view of a static universe that he felt baffled.

Then, in 1929, the astronomer Edwin Hubble

demonstrated that yes, the universe was indeed expanding, with galaxies moving away from one another.
Einstein's equations had been correct.

The year of 1929 also marked Einstein's fiftieth
birthday. He spent it mostly by himself, in a cottage on
a friend's estate, cherishing his privacy. Elsa was dis-
mayed to find him wearing old clothes (she thought she
had hidden them forever) when she and her daughters
came for a small party. With letters and gifts from all
over, his favorite present was a new microscope. Some
of his supporters tried to get the city of Berlin to honor
its most famous citizen by giving him a house in the
country, but anti-Semitic leaders objected. So with his
own money, he ended up buying some property in the
seaside village of Caputh and building a simple wooden
house there.

He was at his happiest while sailing in his new
boat, the *Dolphin*. He didn't swim and liked to court
danger by going out alone without a life jacket, letting
the boat drift while he wrote in his notebooks.

Elsa was on hand to cater to him, serving raspberry
juice and fruit salad. Women friends often dropped by.
As with publicity, Einstein was unable to say no to
flirtation. Elsa was philosophical, saying that what

Nature "gives extravagantly, she takes away extrava-gantly"; with her husband she reluctantly tolerated the bad along with the good. He had a passionate affair with one secretary, even suggesting she move in, before realizing this "triangular geometry" was impossible.

As for his sons, Einstein was at times estranged from them, especially the younger. Eduard wanted to become a psychiatrist and became obsessed with Freud's theories about fathers and sons. After a suicide attempt in 1930, he was diagnosed with schizophrenia and spent the rest of his life in institutions. Einstein be-lieved his son's problems were inherited from Mileva, but he also suspected his presence made Eduard worse, so he stopped visiting his younger son altogether. De-spite rocky moments, he remained in touch with Hans, who became a professor of engineering. Einstein even-tually became close to his two grandsons.

Sigmund Freud, had he gotten Einstein on his couch, might have explored Einstein's problems as a father. That never happened, though Freud was still treating patients in nearby Vienna. Never terribly introspective, Einstein didn't think much of psycho-analysis. "It may not always be helpful to delve into the subconscious. . . . I should very much like to remain in the darkness," he said. He thought Freud had "an often exaggerated faith in his own ideas," and several times refused to cosign Freud's nomination for a Nobel Prize. (Freud never did win one.)

The two did agree on one point—a bleak one. In an exchange of letters about whether war could ever be eliminated, both Freud and Einstein came to the same conclusion: Man was by nature violent.

Einstein mania continued unabated during his second trip to America in 1930. He was offered roles in the movies, met Helen Keller and every other important person in America, and was besieged with requests to lend his name to commercial products (he always refused).

"The reporters asked exquisitely inane questions," he said, "to which I replied with cheap jokes, which were enthusiastically received." Now he was telling reporters it would take three days to give a short definition of theory of relativity.

As a research fellow at the California Institute of Technology, he told the Caltech students to use science to make life better, not worse (as in new weapons)— "Never forget this when you are pondering over your diagrams and equations!" More than almost any other scientist, Einstein used his celebrity to try to do good—for example, promoting world peace. He gave speeches, signed manifestos, joined committees, exchanged letters with other pacifists. "In the old days," he wrote a group of schoolchildren, "peoples spent their lives fearing and even hating one another because of ignorance on all sides." Critics called him impractical and naïve, but he sincerely wanted to help forge a new era. And as rumblings of another world war began, he declared, "I am not only a pacifist, I am a militant pacifist."

Brilliant physicist that he was, Einstein at first completely misjudged the threat of Nazi leader Adolf Hitler. According to Einstein, Hitler would "no longer be important" once the German economy improved.

Meanwhile, the rising Nazi movement was sponsoring conferences to denounce Einstein, the most famous Jew in the world. There were public book burnings of his work, and in 1931 a Nazi-funded book, *One Hundred Authors Against Einstein,* attacked his theory of relativity. Einstein replied that to refute relativity one would not need the word of one hundred scientists, just one fact—which no one had produced.

The cover of a Nazi magazine showed Einstein along with a caption that read "Not Yet Hanged." After a series of death threats, Einstein could no longer live in denial. He and his family were in danger. In December 1932 he decided to leave Germany forever, eventually moving to the United States.

It turned out that Einstein had some enemies in the United States as well. As he was packing to leave, a woman named Mrs. Randolph Frothingham sent a letter to the State Department. On behalf of the Woman Patriot Corporation, she denounced Einstein for pacifism and other beliefs she deemed unpatriotic, recommending denial of his visa. Einstein was amused at first. ("Never yet have I experienced from the fair sex such energetic rejection of all advances.") Then he told the U.S. consulate in Germany that he would come to America only if he was wanted. The State Department did indeed want him and issued the visa promptly. The department opened up a file on him, though, in case unpatriotic "evidence" came to light.

Einstein got out of Germany not a moment too soon. Hitler took power in January 1933, and Nazis promptly raided Einstein's apartment, tearing it apart, then confiscated his seaside cottage and beloved *Dolphin*.

By April, all Jews were banned from teaching in

universities. Hitler declared, "If the dismissal of Jewish scientists means the annihilation of contemporary German science, then we shall do without science for a few years!" In May, more than 40,000 citizens brought books by Jewish authors to a book burning in Berlin, where it was announced, "Jewish intellectualism is dead." Lenard, Einstein's enemy, was named the new chief of Aryan science.

Einstein arrived in the United States with a prestigious job offer in hand. By October, at age fifty-four, Einstein was safely ensconced at the newly formed Institute for Advanced Study at Princeton. (It was near the university but not part of it.) The Institute was designed as a haven for scholars to research history, mathematics, science, and social science without pressure (and without having to teach). Einstein's salary was princely, and his furniture requests were minimal, although one essential he listed was "a large wastebasket, so I can throw away all my mistakes."

He had mixed feelings about America—"a boring and barren society" where frivolous, shallow people seize on "anything that might provide ammunition in the struggle against boredom." But he also adored its freedoms, believing that without freedom there was no creativity in science or anything else.

As events turned darker in Germany, he was aware that friends and relatives still there were in danger. Many, such as Uncle Jakob's grown son and his family, would soon perish in the Holocaust. Einstein spent time fund-raising for Jewish refugees and personally helped to pay for scores of Jews to come to the United States.

He bought a simple white house at 112 Mercer Street. He'd start off each morning with a bubble bath and two fried eggs, then start out on the two-mile walk to his office at the Institute. He'd come home for a macaroni lunch, but if lost in thought, would forget to eat and mosey back to the Institute on an empty stomach.

Einstein was a hot topic among his neighbors, who got a kick out of living next door to a colorful eccentric. They whispered about how he couldn't drive a car (he found it too complicated), his weird clothes (cotton sweatshirts, baggy corduroy pants, and no socks—too annoying when the big toe poked a hole in the top) . . . and that he admitted to never wearing pajamas! ("When I retire, I sleep as nature made me.") He also became famous in the neighborhood for playing the violin and helping kids with their math, sometimes heating up cans of beans for guests or serving cookies baked by Elsa.

From the world at large he received floods of letters, many from children; often he wrote back. His office at home, overlooking the garden, had the usual easy chair, wall-to-wall bookcases, portraits of Maxwell, Newton, and his newest hero, Mahatma Gandhi, the nonviolent leader in the fight for India's independence. Einstein lived and worked in Princeton for his final twenty years, with numerous pets, taken care of by Elsa (until her death in 1936) and then by assorted women friends.

He was so well-known that people on the street would stop and ask for an explanation of "that theory." He finally devised a method of escaping strangers: "Pardon me, sorry! Always I am mistaken for Professor Einstein."

He sailed on, thinking about his unified field theory, trying and quitting various approaches. "I live like a bear in my cave."

CHAPTER TWELVE

Investigated by the FBI

"EOPLE LIKE YOU and me never grow old," Einstein wrote to a scientist friend. "We never cease to stand like curious children before the great mystery into which we were born." The wonder he'd felt as a child playing with a compass never left him.

J. Robert Oppenheimer, soon to become known as the father of the atom bomb, met Einstein in 1935 and wrote, "There was always with him a wonderful purity at once childlike and profoundly stubborn." Apparently this could be maddening, as Oppenheimer also said jokingly, "Einstein is completely cuckoo."

Younger physicists were happy to come and help out Einstein. He relied on them to do the math—what one called the "dirty work"—while he would pace and mutter, "I vill a little t'ink" (he never conquered English).

In 1935 he published his final important paper, four pages called "Can the Quantum-Mechanical Description of Physical Reality Be Regarded as Complete?" This mouthful of a title was another attack on quantum mechanics. In his later years, he stopped opposing the theory and simply tried to incorporate it into his unified field theory.

Einstein was never rich (and didn't care). But *The Evolution of Physics,* a 1938 book coauthored with a colleague, was a hit, making him financially secure.

By then, to his horror, physicists were seriously pursuing whether his equation $E = mc^2$, which saw mass and energy as forms of the same thing, might help lead to the creation of an atomic bomb. Einstein had been dismissing the idea—it was true that the small amount of matter in an atom was the equivalent of a great deal of energy. But there was no simple way to release the energy. But now scientists were asking, What if you bombarded an atom with particles and split it into separate atoms? Would that release some of the energy that held the atom together? Einstein remained skeptical. As late as 1934, he remain convinced that "Splitting the atom by bombardment is something akin to shooting birds in the dark in a place where there are only a few birds."

In March of 1939, his sparring partner Niels Bohr paid him a visit and broke the news: A group of German scientists had discovered nuclear fission. Bombarding a uranium atom with neutrons, they had succeeded in splitting the atom, creating two new atoms with slightly less mass. The small amount of lost mass was released as energy.

Einstein still wasn't alarmed. One split atom released only a limited amount of energy. But then in July 1939, Hungarian physicist Leo Szilard (who had once invented a refrigerator with Einstein) presented Einstein with a horrifying thought: It might be possible to create a "chain reaction" where splitting an atom once would cause more atoms to split, which in turn would cause even more to split, and so on. A chain reaction would release an enormous amount of energy. How much? Einstein's equation $E = mc^2$ predicted exactly how much . . . enough to obliterate a whole city or even more.

Einstein was definitely alarmed now. With Szilard,

he sent a letter urging U.S. President Franklin Roosevelt to develop an atomic bomb. The Germans, under Hitler's rule, were already working on one. America had to start researching the idea now. Nothing was more important than this race. The Nazis must not win it.

Einstein was the world's most famous scientist. He was also a famous pacifist. Yet now he was pushing for the creation of the deadliest weapon in history. His flipflopping on the issue may have made some people think less of him, but as Szilard pointed out, "The one thing most scientists are really afraid of is to make fools of themselves. Einstein was free from such a fear."

Also, in the true spirit of scientific thinking, Einstein felt free to change his mind on any subject when presented with new evidence. He came to the conclusion that pacifism was not absolute but a concept to be reexamined. So great was the threat to civilization from Nazi aggression that Einstein split with his pacifist friends. He decided that military aggression was the lesser of two evils. He even admitted that if he were young, he'd join the army to fight the Nazis.

Einstein signed the famous letter about the atomic bomb on August 2, 1939. World War II broke out later that month, after Germany invaded Poland. Einstein's letter did not actually reach Roosevelt until October 11. An aide read it aloud to make sure it got the president's full attention. That very night, Roosevelt organized the Briggs Committee to study the use of uranium chain reactions to create a weapon. But the committee moved very slowly; to them the possibility of an atom bomb seemed remote.

In March 1940, the same year he became a proud American citizen, Einstein helped with a second, more urgent letter, raising the issue of Germany's progress developing a bomb. In response, Roosevelt called a meeting and invited Einstein, who declined, replying that he had a cold. He had no desire to take an active role in this deadly project. And even if he had wanted to, he might have been rejected as a security risk; J. Edgar Hoover, director of the Federal Bureau of Investigation, had already reported that Einstein would never be "a loyal American citizen" because of his past associations with pacifist organizations.

The Manhattan Project was the name of the ultra-secret effort begun in early December of 1941 to develop the first atomic bomb. And on December 7, 1941, the United States officially entered the war after the Japanese bombing of Pearl Harbor, a naval base in Hawaii, resulted in the death of 2,400 Americans.

Many of Einstein's former physicist colleagues, having fled from Germany and other countries under Hitler's control, became part of the Manhattan Project. Despite its name, the project's headquarters was in the desert town of Los Alamos, New Mexico. The most intense science project in history, it would cost billions and employ some 130,000 people. Einstein was not asked to participate and was kept out of the loop because of fears about his loyalty and his own obvious unwillingness.

Einstein did help with less sensitive issues related to the war. He consulted with the U.S. Navy to check for flaws in new designs for weapons (much like his old job at the patent office). He also donated the money from the auction of a handwritten copy of his 1905 paper on special relativity to the Allied cause. It sold in 1944 for $6.5 million.

As the war dragged on and the work of the Manhattan Project progressed, Einstein was becoming increasingly frantic that no one was considering how to *control* atomic weapons once they were invented. He wrote yet another impassioned letter to Roosevelt about this. It was found in the president's office after his death in April 1945.

Four months later, the United States dropped

atomic bombs on the Japanese cities of Hiroshima
(August 6) and Nagasaki (August 9). The bombs in-
stantly killed more than a hundred thousand people and
inflicted deadly radiation sickness on many thousands
more. The Japanese surrendered days later. On August
15, 1945, World War II was over. After learning of the
bombings, Einstein remained silent and depressed for
weeks.

Even though the bombings helped end the war, Einstein found it unbearable that his work had played any
part in such horrific destruction. The bomb was the exact opposite of what he saw as the purpose of science.

As for the Nazis and all the talk about their cam-
paign to build a bomb—it was overhyped. It turned out
that Nazi physicists had decided that a big-enough bomb
could probably not be developed. They had not devoted
a lot of time or money to it. Nor was the necessary brain
power assembled. (Many of the best physicists had fled
from Germany to America.)

Einstein aged rapidly in the aftermath of the war.
Almost immediately he formed and headed the Emergency Committee of Atomic Scientists, working toward world peace and against any future use of nuclear
weapons. He pushed for a unifying world government

that would impose strict controls on nuclear technology. The United Nations, formed in October 1945, fell far short of what he envisioned.

"We drift toward unparalleled catastrophe," Einstein declared. When he was asked what a Third World War would be like, he couldn't say beyond knowing that modern civilization would be obliterated, adding, "But I can tell you what [weapons] they will use in the Fourth—rocks."

In part he was returning to his earlier faith in pacifism; in part he was reacting to guilt over the role his work had played in creating the bomb. Although the media frequently played up the connection, he insisted, "I do not consider myself the father of the release of atomic energy." He called his first letter to Roosevelt "the greatest mistake of my life." Einstein went on to be drawn to various social justice causes in America, especially advancing the civil rights of African Americans. When Princeton hotels refused the black singer Marian Anderson a room, for example, she was always welcome to stay at the Einstein home on Mercer Street.

By now just about everything he did attracted the keen interest of the FBI. Postwar tensions between America and Soviet Russia put the FBI on high alert

for Russian spies in the United States. The list of suspects included anyone who might be at all sympathetic
to Communist beliefs and anyone who criticized the
government, as Einstein did. The State Department file
on Einstein grew enormous—1,427 pages of documents.
Ironically, Einstein did have a four-year affair with a
woman who *was* a Soviet spy. The FBI never found out
about this. (Their letters became public in 1998.)

Although the U.S. government had serious misgiv-
ings about Einstein's character, the fledgling state of Israel had no such reservations. He is perhaps the only
scientist ever asked to become president of a country. In
1952, David Ben-Gurion, Israel's premier, offered Einstein the post of president of the State of Israel, formed
just four years earlier in 1948. Einstein respectfully
declined. "I lack both the natural aptitude and the experience to deal properly with people," he said percep-
tively.

He officially retired from the Institute for Advanced
Study at age sixty-six, but continued to walk there every day, holding papers of notes scribbled the night before. He often walked with close friends, having deep
conversations about politics, religion, and physics.

On his seventieth birthday, his friends delighted

him with a record player and AM-FM radio. Music was still his love.

He kept publishing articles attempting to work toward the unified field theory. But if anything, physics seemed less unified than ever, as new particles and forces were discovered. Several times he felt like he was on the right track at last, only to be derailed. No longer could he come up with a useful thought experiment, as he'd been able to do in the past. But he never quite gave up: "I feel like a kid who cannot get the hang of the ABCs, even though, strangely enough, I do not abandon hope." The work was valuable regardless of the outcome: "The search for truth is more precious than its possession."

He hoped to bequeath the problem to younger brains to explore, though he worried that the existing political climate in the United States would stifle free scientific exploration. Einstein was horrified by the growing influence of Joseph McCarthy, a senator from Wisconsin on a witch hunt for suspected American Communists. McCarthy's accusations often had little basis in fact, yet they ruined many people's reputations and careers. Einstein said about McCarthy's supporters, "The rule of the dimwitted is unparalleled because there are so many of them and their votes count just as much as ours."

He felt duty-bound to speak out, because he believed that this atmosphere of fear prevented younger scientists from thinking independently. He went so far as to say that if he were young and living in America, he'd be a plumber rather than a scientist or scholar: "Everything—even lunacy—is mass-produced here."

By this time he was well into his seventies, an old man. Years earlier, he'd been diagnosed with a faulty blood vessel in his stomach that could burst at any time, killing him. (He refused experimental surgery that might prolong his life, wanting to die "elegantly.") So for years he'd been living with a ticking bomb.

In the last week of his life, at age seventy-six, he and ten other scientists signed the Einstein-Russell Manifesto, calling for nations to prevent World War III by settling conflicts peacefully, warning that further developments in bombs would destroy the human race.

On April 18, 1955, the vessel finally burst. Einstein's body was found surrounded by twelve pages of notes. On them were scribbled equations for his Theory of Everything.

CHAPTER THIRTEEN

Why He Stands Alone

INSTEIN'S GENERAL THEORY of relativity has been called "probably the greatest scientific discovery ever made" by Paul Dirac, a fellow Nobel Prize winner in physics. Einstein gave science a whole new way of looking at reality, at the relationship between matter, motion, time, space, and energy.

No experiments have ever proven relativity wrong, and no one questions it anymore. Just in the last few decades, more confirming evidence has piled up now that we have ever-more-accurate instruments—space satellites, lasers, supercomputers, atomic clocks so superprecise they can measure time in nanoseconds (illustrating how speed really does make time slow down).

For the theory of relativity, and for jump-starting quantum theory in physics, Einstein's is the most famous name in science. His work continues to win Nobel Prizes for physicists who came after him.

Dozens of biographies in the past several years attest to the continuing fascination with the man with the soulful eyes and crazy hair. Steven Spielberg used Einstein's eyes as a model for those of his lovable alien in *E.T.: The Extra-Terrestrial*. Still a synonym for "genius," his name is even incorporated in commercial products, such as Disney's "Baby Einstein" line of books and toys. Einstein has an asteroid named after him, an opera, a ballet, a medical syndrome (describing children who talk late), even a BMX maneuver—the Einstein flip.

For such a superstar, Einstein's *work* is probably the least understood of any of the giants of science. It *is* mind-bendingly difficult. And unlike Darwin and evolution or Curie and radiation, it is harder to describe what he discovered—he simply changed notions of space and time.

You can point to many areas of life today that show

his influence—nuclear power, fiber optics, space travel. You can list things that wouldn't be here without him. TV would have been impossible without his work on the photoelectric effect, for example. Quantum theory led to the invention of so many modern electronics— cell phones, computers, lasers, barcode scanners, smoke alarms, the red exit signs in malls and theaters, and medical devices like PET scans for finding tumors. GPS systems use his $E = mc^2$ equation to take into account the effects of speed and gravity.

Hot topics of research continue to flow from Einstein's work—for example, black holes (predicted by the general theory of relativity and later identified by the Hubble Space Telescope); the Big Bang (the theory about the origin of the universe, which derives directly from the general theory of relativity); the force we call "dark energy" that speeds up the expansion of the universe.

Today physics is actually trendy. The percentage of high-school students taking physics courses is at an all-time high, and at the college level the number of bachelor's degrees awarded in physics has grown by 31 percent since 2000. In advanced physics there is much more collaboration, with teams of scientists working together on problems. In 2008 the attention of eight

thousand physicists turned to the Large Hadron Collider, near Geneva, Switzerland—and the ongoing investigation of Einstein's theories.

Science may seem to have less room now for reclusive outsiders, a development Einstein would not have liked: "It is important to foster individuality, for only the individual can produce the new ideas."

So many questions still to be explored, new connections in the universe to make—we clearly need more Einsteins to help us see the whole picture. "Nature shows us only the tail of the lion," he once said, "but I do not doubt that the lion belongs to it, even though he cannot at once reveal himself because of his enormous size."

His relentless pursuit of connections continues to amaze: he spent ten years on his special theory of relativity, eight on the general theory of relativity, more than thirty on the unified field theory.

Until recently, most scientists dismissed the work of those last thirty years of his life as unimportant— some say he could have spent it sailing and the world would be no poorer. But Einstein himself was more optimistic about the value of his late work. He said, "I will be dead for quite some time before my current work is appreciated."

And indeed physicists continue working on Einstein's ultimate dream of a Theory of Everything—an ambitious explanation of the whole cosmos. Today the leading theory up for debate is string theory, which assumes that everything in the universe is made of tiny strings vibrating in various ways. Einstein might have appreciated the theory's echo of the violin strings he loved so much.

He would continue to advise: "The important thing is not to stop questioning. Curiosity has its own reason for existing."

Curiosity drove Albert Einstein all his life. And because of his curiosity, he changed how we understand the world.

SOURCES

Starred—young readers

"Albert Einstein: Image and Impact," The American Institute of Physics, http://www.aip.org/history/einstein/

Albert Einstein Online, http://www.westegg.com/einstein/

Bodanis, David. *E = mc²: A Biography of the World's Most Famous Equation.* New York: Walker & Company, 2000.

* Brown, Don. *Odd Boy Out: Young Albert Einstein.* Boston: Houghton Mifflin, 2004.

Calaprice, Alice. *The Einstein Almanac.* Baltimore: Johns Hopkins University Press, 2005.

Calaprice, Alice, ed. *The Expanded Quotable Einstein.* Princeton: Princeton University Press, 2005.

* Delano, Marfe Ferguson. *Genius: A Photobiography of Albert Einstein.* Washington, D.C.: National Geographic Children's Books, 2005.

"Einstein," American Museum of Natural History, http://www.amnh.org/exhibitions/einstein/

Einstein Archives Online, http://www.alberteinstein.info/

Einstein Papers Project, http://www.einstein.caltech.edu/index.html

SOURCES

* "Einstein for Young Readers," Albert Einstein Archives, Hebrew University of Jerusalem, http://www.albert-einstein.org/.index6

"Einstein's Big Idea," NOVA, http://www.pbs.org/wgbh/nova /einstein/

* Hakim, Joy. *Einstein Adds a New Dimension*. Washington, D.C.: Smithsonian, 2007.

Isaacson, Walter. *Einstein: His Life and Universe*. New York: Simon and Schuster, 2007.

Kaku, Michio. *Einstein's Cosmos: How Albert Einstein's Vision Transformed Our Understanding of Space and Time*. New York: W.W. Norton, 2004.

* Macleod, Elizabeth. *Albert Einstein: A Life of Genius*. Toronto: Kids Can Press, 2003.

* Meltzer, Milton. *Albert Einstein: A Biography*. New York: Holiday House, 2007.

Neffe, Jürgen. *Einstein: A Biography*. New York: Farrar, Straus & Giroux, 2007.

Overbye, Dennis. *Einstein in Love: A Scientific Romance*. New York: Viking, 2000.

Pais, Abraham. *Einstein Lived Here*. Oxford: Oxford University Press, 1994.

INDEX